# CKD
# Stage 3
# Cookbook for Seniors

*Savor Tasty and Nutritious Meals for Better Health*

*Elva H. Miller*

# Contents

Introduction........................................................................................6

    Angie's Journey to Kidney-Friendly Cooking................................6

    What This Book Is About..............................................................7

    Who Does This Book Help?...........................................................8

    Our Mission: To Help You Achieve Better Health.........................8

Chapter 1........................................................................................ 10

Background Of CKD...................................................................... 10

    Understanding CKD Stage 3...................................................... 10

    The Importance of Diet in Managing CKD................................ 10

    Tips for Seniors to Follow a Kidney-Friendly Diet......................11

    Adopting a Kidney-Friendly Lifestyle....................................... 12

Chapter 2........................................................................................ 14

Healthy and Delicious Kidney-Friendly Recipes........................... 14

    Breakfast Recipes..................................................................... 14

    Lunch Recipes..........................................................................24

    Dinner Recipes........................................................................ 34

Chapter 3........................................................................................ 46

    Mouth Watering Snack and Dessert Recipes............................. 46

    Soups and Stews Recipes.......................................................... 56

Chapter 4........................................................................................ 64

    Smoothies & Drinks Recipes.................................................... 64

    Vegetables and Sides Recipes.................................................... 70

    Main Dishes............................................................................. 78

Chapter 5........................................................................................ 88

Tips and Resources....................................................................... 88

    Grocery Shopping Guide for CKD............................................88

14-Day Meal Plan for CKD Stage 3.................................................................89

Cooking Tips for Seniors..............................................................................91

Managing Portion Sizes...............................................................................92

Conversion Charts For Measuring Ingredients............................................92

Practical Tips for Using Conversion Tables................................................ 93

**Conclusion**............................................................................................. 94

**Bonus Section**..........................................................................................96

# Introduction

## Angie's Journey to Kidney-Friendly Cooking

Angie was always the heart and soul of her family's kitchen. She enjoyed trying out new recipes and watching the excitement on her family's faces as they devoured her culinary creations. However, Angie just received news that caused her to pause: she was diagnosed with Stage 3 chronic kidney illness.

Her doctor encouraged her to follow a kidney-friendly diet, emphasizing meals with low salt, potassium, and phosphorus levels. Angie felt overwhelmed. She did not know where to begin. How could she create dinners that matched these rigorous dietary criteria while also being entertaining for her family?

One evening, while searching the internet for kidney-friendly meals, she came across a community forum where individuals discussed their challenges and accomplishments with CKD diets. One name kept appearing: **"CKD Stage 3 Cookbook for Seniors"**. Angie was intrigued and decided to read the positive reviews. People appreciated the book for its simple recipes and excellent meals that their entire family enjoyed.

Angie, determined to try it, ordered the book. When it arrived, she eagerly turned the pages, feeling a glimmer of hope. The opening was reassuring, describing CKD in simple words and highlighting the importance of food in managing the disease. Angie believed that the authors understood her difficulties.

Her first challenge was breakfast. She chose to try the Low Sodium Vegetable Omelet. The recipe was simple, with clear directions and a short list of components. Angie was relieved to find that she had the majority of the ingredients in her pantry. As she prepared, the perfume of fresh vegetables and herbs filled the kitchen. She gave the omelet to her family, who were initially hesitant but eventually gobbled it, complimenting its flavor. Angie couldn't help smiling.

Then she tackled lunch. The Grilled Chicken Quinoa Salad drew her attention. The bright colors and promise of a healthful dinner were irresistible. The cookbook included a step-by-step tutorial, making it simple for Angie to prepare the dish. Her family adored it, particularly the acidic homemade dressing, which was both kidney-friendly and delicious.

Dinner was the real test. Angie chose Baked Salmon with Herb Sauce. The cookbook's advice on preparing fish to reduce salt and phosphorus was invaluable. The dish was a smash, with her family requesting seconds. Angie felt a sense of accomplishment—she was not only managing her health, but also delivering joy to her loved ones.

As the weeks progressed into months, Angie tried more recipes from the booklet. She discovered new favorites, such as Apple

Cinnamon Pancakes for breakfast and Lemon Garlic Chicken for dinner. The book's variety kept mealtimes interesting. Even desserts, such as Baked Apples with Cinnamon, were something her family looked forward to.

Angie particularly loved the practical portions on meal planning, grocery shopping, and senior-friendly cooking techniques. These suggestions made her cooking adventures easier and more fun.

One day, at a family gathering, her sister said, "Angie, you've always cooked better! "What is your secret?" Angie grinned and said, "It's this incredible book, **"CKD Stage 3 Cookbook for Seniors."** It has made all the difference for me."

Her narrative circulated among friends and family, and many were moved by her experience. They witnessed how Angie had improved her diet without sacrificing taste or satisfaction. The cookbook had become her trusted companion, guiding her through her health issues while still sharing great meals with her loved ones.

If you or someone you know has been diagnosed with Stage 3 CKD, this cookbook can help you navigate the process. **"CKD Stage 3 Cookbook for Seniors"** provides a source of comfort and inspiration in the kitchen. With its simple recipes and practical advice, it guarantees that every dinner is both kidney-friendly and enjoyable for the whole family. Embrace your journey to greater health with confidence and flavor.

## Welcome To This Book "CKD Stage 3 Cookbook for Seniors"

This cookbook is a thorough handbook that addresses the specific dietary demands of seniors with Stage 3 chronic kidney disease (CKD). Our purpose is to give you the tools, knowledge, and recipes you need to effectively manage your condition while also enjoying great, gratifying meals.

## What This Book Is About

This cookbook is more than simply a compilation of dishes; it's a guide to understanding and navigating the dietary restrictions that come with CKD Stage 3. Inside, you can find:

- ❖ *Detailed Information on CKD Stage 3:* Learn about CKD Stage 3, how it affects your health, and the vital role diet plays in controlling your illness.
- ❖ *Dietary Guidelines:* Learn about the necessity of controlling sodium, potassium, and phosphorus in your diet and how to do so through sensible food choices.
- ❖ *Practical Tips:* Learn how to plan meals, buy groceries, and prepare with elders in mind.
- ❖ *Nutritional and Delicious Recipes:* Explore a variety of kidney-friendly meals that are simple to prepare and enjoy, including breakfast, supper, snacks, and desserts.

## Who Does This Book Help?

This cookbook is specifically designed for:

- ❖ *Seniors with CKD Stage 3:* Tailored to fit the dietary demands of seniors, ensuring that meals are not only kidney-friendly but also simple to prepare and consume.
- ❖ *Family and Caregivers:* Offering advice and recipes that can be shared with loved ones, making it easier to assist elderly in managing their nutritional needs.
- ❖ *Anyone Seeking Kidney Health:* Whether you have CKD Stage 3 or simply want to keep your kidneys healthy, this book offers useful ideas and delicious recipes that promote general well-being.

## How Can This Book Help You?

Navigating the dietary restrictions of CKD Stage 3 can be difficult, but this cookbook will help you every step of the way. Here's how.

- ❖ *Simplified Cooking:* With simple directions and easy-to-find ingredients, you can confidently make meals that are specifically designed to support kidney health.
- ❖ *Balanced nourishment:* Each recipe is meticulously designed to balance important nutrients while reducing detrimental ones, ensuring that you receive the nourishment you require without jeopardizing your health.

- ❖ *Variation and Flavor:* Enjoy a variety of delectable and satisfying meals, demonstrating that a kidney-friendly diet does not need to be boring or monotonous.
- ❖ *Empowerment through Knowledge:* Give yourself the knowledge to make informed food decisions, allowing you to take charge of your health.

## Our Mission: To Help You Achieve Better Health

Our purpose for this cookbook is simple: to help seniors with CKD Stage 3 live better, more enjoyable lives via eating. We think that food is more than just nourishment; it can bring joy, connection, and healing. By giving you this detailed information, we hope to enhance your quality of life and support your health journey by providing nutritious and enjoyable meals.

We hope that this book will become a reliable kitchen companion, guiding you to improved health with each meal you create.

*Thank You For Letting Us Be A Part Of Your Wellness Journey.*

*Let's Take This Journey Together, Appreciating Every Delicious And Nutritious Bite.*

# Chapter 1

# Background Of CKD

## Understanding CKD Stage 3

Chronic kidney disease (CKD) affects millions of individuals globally, primarily seniors. CKD is defined as a steady decline of renal function over time. It goes through five phases, the third showing moderate renal injury. At this point, it is critical to take preventive measures to control the condition and slow its course.

A glomerular filtration rate (GFR) of 30 to 59 mL/min indicates CKD Stage 3. This rate indicates how well your kidneys remove waste and extra fluids from your blood. A GFR in this range indicates that your kidneys are not operating properly, which can lead to an accumulation of waste products in your body, resulting in a variety of health problems.

## Symptoms & Diagnosis:

Many persons with CKD Stage 3 may not have any visible symptoms. However, some typical symptoms include weariness, edema in the legs and ankles, altered urine patterns, and high blood pressure. It is frequently detected with blood tests that assess GFR and urine tests that look for albumin, a protein that leaks into the urine when the kidneys are injured.

Early detection and regular monitoring are critical in controlling CKD. Your doctor may propose routine testing to monitor kidney function and alter treatment strategies accordingly. Understanding the implications of CKD Stage 3 is the first step toward successful management.

## The Importance of Diet in Managing CKD

Diet is critical in controlling CKD, particularly in Stage 3. The basic objectives are to lessen the workload on the kidneys, maintain sufficient nutrition, and avoid additional renal injury. Here are some important dietary recommendations for those with CKD Stage 3:

*1. Sodium:* Reducing salt consumption is critical for treating CKD. Excess sodium can cause high blood pressure, fluid retention, and more kidney injury. Aim to consume fewer than 2,300 mg of sodium each day. This means eliminating processed foods, canned soups, and salty snacks in favor of fresh, complete foods.

*2. Potassium:* Potassium is a vital mineral, but too much can be detrimental to people with CKD. High potassium levels can cause hazardous cardiac arrhythmias. Concentrate on low-potassium foods like apples, berries, carrots, and green beans, and restrict high-potassium meals like bananas, oranges, potatoes, and tomatoes.

*3. Phosphorus:* Managing phosphorus intake is similarly crucial. Excess phosphorus can weaken bones and damage the heart and blood vessels. Choose foods low in phosphorus, such as fresh fruits and vegetables, rice, and pasta. Avoid processed meals, dairy products, nuts, and seeds, as they are generally high in phosphorus.

**4. *Protein:*** While protein is essential for overall health, too much protein can strain the kidneys. Moderation is crucial. Choose high-quality protein sources such as lean meats, fish, eggs, and plant-based alternatives like beans and lentils. Your healthcare professional or nutritionist can assist you in determining the proper protein amount for your needs.

**5. *Fluids:*** Fluid intake must be adjusted to avoid fluid excess, which can result in edema and high blood pressure. Your healthcare practitioner will advise you on the amount of fluids you should consume based on your specific condition and needs.

## Tips for Seniors to Follow a Kidney-Friendly Diet

Adhering to a kidney-friendly diet can be difficult, but with the appropriate tactics, it is completely doable. Here are some practical recommendations to help elderly maintain a balanced diet while living with CKD Stage III:

**1. *Plan your meals:*** Meal planning is vital for treating chronic kidney disease. Plan your weekly meals and snacks, with an emphasis on kidney-friendly items. Make a grocery list based on your meal plan to ensure you have everything you need. This can assist you avoid making impulse purchases for unhealthy meals.

**2. *Read the Food Labels:*** Become an expert label reader. Check the nutritional information on packaged foods for salt, potassium, and phosphorus levels. Look for products marked "low sodium," "no added salt," or "low potassium."

**3. *Cook at home:*** Preparing meals at home allows you complete control over the ingredients and cooking methods. Experiment with herbs and spices to boost taste without adding salt. Cooking at home also allows you to customize dishes to suit your dietary requirements.

**4. *Select Fresh Foods:*** Fresh, whole foods often have less salt, potassium, and phosphorus than processed and packaged foods. Consume plenty of fruits, vegetables, lean proteins, and whole grains in your diet.

**5. *Hydrate wisely:*** While staying hydrated is key, it's also critical not to overdo it. Follow your healthcare provider's fluid intake guidelines. Drink fluids throughout the day rather than in big quantities at once.

**6. *Seek Support:*** Don't be afraid to seek help from family, friends, or a nutritionist. They can offer support, assist with food preparation, and give vital advice. Joining a chronic kidney disease support group might also be beneficial.

**7. *Managing Portions:*** Portion control is essential in treating CKD. Use smaller dishes and bowls to keep portion proportions under control. Eating smaller, more frequent meals might also help you manage hunger and stay energized.

**8. Track Your Health:** Regular check-ups with your healthcare professional are essential. They can monitor your kidney function, make dietary changes as needed, and address any concerns you may have. Keep a food journal to document your eating habits and how they affect your health.

**9. Experiment with Recipes:** Do not be hesitant to test new recipes and ingredients. A diversified diet can help you avoid meal fatigue and acquire a wide range of nutrients. This cookbook contains a multitude of kidney-friendly dishes that will keep your meals interesting and enjoyable.

**10. Be Positive:** Keeping a cheerful mindset is vital. Adjusting to a new diet might be difficult, but with time and experience, it gets easier. Celebrate your accomplishments, no matter how minor, and keep focused on your health objectives.

## Adopting a Kidney-Friendly Lifestyle

Living with CKD Stage 3 necessitates careful nutritional choices, but this does not mean you have to forgo flavor or enjoyment. By adopting a kidney-friendly lifestyle, you may regain control of your health and quality of life. This cookbook is intended to help you on your journey, with tasty, nutritious meals that are simple to make and enjoy.

Remember that controlling CKD is a marathon, not a sprint. Every positive change you make, no matter how tiny, improves your overall well-being. With the correct knowledge, tools, and support, you can thrive while living with Stage 3 CKD.

# Chapter 2

## Healthy and Delicious Kidney-Friendly Recipes

## Breakfast Recipes

### 1. Apple Cinnamon Pancake

These fluffy apple cinnamon pancakes provide a delightful and satisfying meal that is also good for your kidneys.

These pancakes, bursting with the sweet flavor of apples and toasty spices, are an ideal way to start the day. While conventional pancakes might be heavy in potassium and phosphorus, this dish has been carefully modified to meet the dietary requirements of those with CKD stage 3.

- ❖ *Preparation time: 10 minutes*
- ❖ *Cook time: 15 minutes.*
- ❖ *Total time: 25 minutes.*

**Ingredients:**

- ❖ 1 cup low potassium pancake mix
- ❖ 1 egg white.
- ❖ 1/2 cup of unsweetened almond milk.
- ❖ 1/4 cup applesauce, unsweetened
- ❖ 1/4 teaspoon of ground cinnamon.
- ❖ 1/4 teaspoon baking powder.
- ❖ Pinch of salt.
- ❖ Optional: sugar replacement (to taste).

**Instructions:**

- ❖ In a large mixing bowl, combine the pancake mix, egg white, almond milk, applesauce, cinnamon, baking powder, salt, and sugar replacement (if using).
- ❖ Cook in a lightly oiled griddle or frying pan over medium heat.
- ❖ Pour 1/4 cup batter onto a heated griddle for each pancake.
- ❖ Cook until bubbles appear on the surface and the sides have set, then flip and cook until golden brown.
- ❖ Serve immediately with your preferred low-potassium toppings, such as maple syrup or sugar-free whipped cream.

*Serving size: two pancakes.*

**Nutrition Facts (approximate per serving):**

- ❖ Calories: 150.
- ❖ Carbohydrate: 25 grams
- ❖ Fat: 3g

- ❖ Cholesterol: 0 mg.
- ❖ Sodium: 100 mg.
- ❖ Potassium: 150 mg.
- ❖ Phosphorus: 50 mg.
- ❖ Protein: 5 grams.
- ❖ Fiber: 2 grams.

## Cooking Tips:

- ❖ For added taste, try adding ground nutmeg or cardamom to the batter.
- ❖ Allowing the batter to rest for a few minutes before cooking will result in exceptionally fluffy pancakes.
- ❖ Serve with fresh berries or a dollop of Greek yogurt for extra nutrition.

## Health Benefits:

- ❖ Apples include fiber, which promotes digestive health.
- ❖ Cinnamon has been demonstrated to help regulate blood sugar levels.
- ❖ Pancakes with low potassium content can help manage CKD.
- ❖ Remember to ask your doctor or a qualified nutritionist for specialized nutritional recommendations.

## 2. Spinach & Mushroom Scramble

This Spinach and Mushroom Scramble is a substantial and nutritious breakfast or lunch choice ideal for people with stage 3 chronic kidney disease. This dish is high in protein, iron, and fiber, making it a fulfilling supper for those following dietary restrictions. The mix of earthy mushrooms and lush spinach results in a tasty and nutritious dinner.

- ❖ *Preparation time: 5 minutes*
- ❖ *Cooking time: 10 minutes.*
- ❖ *Total time: 15 minutes.*

## Ingredients:

- ❖ 2 big egg whites.
- ❖ 1/4 cup reduced sodium cottage cheese
- ❖ 1/4 cup chopped onion.
- ❖ 1/4 cup sliced mushrooms.

- ❖ 1 cup of fresh spinach, chopped
- ❖ 1 tablespoon of olive oil.
- ❖ Add salt and pepper to taste.

## Instructions:

- ❖ In a mixing dish, combine egg whites and cottage cheese and stir until smooth.
- ❖ In a nonstick skillet, heat olive oil over medium heat.
- ❖ Cook the onions and mushrooms in the skillet for about 5 minutes, or until softened.
- ❖ Add the spinach and simmer for about 1 minute, or until wilted.
- ❖ Pour the egg white mixture over the vegetable mixture and scramble for 5 minutes, or until thoroughly cooked.
- ❖ Season with salt and pepper to taste.

### Serving Size: One serving

**Nutrition Facts (approximate per serving):**

- ❖ Calories: 120.
- ❖ Carbs: 3g
- ❖ Fat: 7g
- ❖ Cholesterol: 0 mg.
- ❖ Sodium: 150 mg.
- ❖ Potassium: 200 mg.
- ❖ Phosphorus: 80 mg.
- ❖ Protein: 12 grams.
- ❖ Fiber: 2 grams.

## Cooking Tips:

- ❖ To enhance taste, add garlic powder or dried oregano to the scramble.
- ❖ To round up the meal, serve with whole-grain toast.
- ❖ To minimize potassium, carefully rinse raw spinach before use.

## Health Benefits:

- ❖ Spinach is rich in iron, which aids in oxygen transfer.
- ❖ Mushrooms are high in potassium and low in salt. They also contain antioxidants.
- ❖ Egg whites are high in protein and low in cholesterol, unlike entire eggs.
- ❖ Remember to ask your doctor or a qualified nutritionist for specialized nutritional recommendations.

## 3. Quinoa Breakfast Bowl.

Quinoa Breakfast Bowl is a protein and fiber-rich meal. This recipe is ideal for people with CKD stage 3, since it provides a tasty way to start the day while adhering to dietary restrictions. The combination of quinoa, fresh vegetables, and a touch of protein results in a well-balanced and tasty breakfast.

- ❖ **Preparation time: 10 minutes**
- ❖ **Cook time: 15 minutes.**
- ❖ **Total time: 25 minutes.**

**Ingredients:**

- ❖ 1/2 cup of quinoa, rinsed
- ❖ 1 cup water.
- ❖ 1/4 cup chopped onion.
- ❖ 1/4 cup diced bell pepper.
- ❖ 1/4 cup chopped spinach.
- ❖ 2 tablespoons of chopped fresh parsley.
- ❖ 1 tablespoon of olive oil.

- ❖ 2 tablespoons of reduced-fat feta cheese (optional).
- ❖ Add salt and pepper to taste.

**Instructions:**

- ❖ Rinse the quinoa thoroughly with cold water.
- ❖ In a small saucepan, mix the quinoa and water. Bring to a boil, then lower to a low heat, cover, and cook for 15 minutes, or until all the water is absorbed.
- ❖ While the quinoa cooks, heat olive oil in a skillet over medium heat. Cook for about 5 minutes, or until the onion and bell pepper soften.
- ❖ Add the spinach and simmer for about 1 minute, or until wilted.
- ❖ In a mixing bowl, combine the cooked quinoa with the vegetable combination and parsley.
- ❖ Season with salt and pepper to taste.
- ❖ Sprinkle with crumbled feta cheese (optional).

*Serving Size: One serving*

**Nutrition Facts (approximate per serving):**

- ❖ Calories: 180
- ❖ Carbohydrate: 25 grams
- ❖ Fat: 5g
- ❖ Cholesterol: 0 mg.
- ❖ Sodium: 150 mg.
- ❖ Potassium: 200 mg.
- ❖ Phosphorus: 100 mg.
- ❖ Protein: 6 grams.
- ❖ Fiber: 3 grams.

**Cooking Tips:**

- ❖ For a warm breakfast, pair the quinoa bowl with a fried egg.
- ❖ Experiment with other vegetables including zucchini, mushrooms, and tomatoes.
- ❖ Sprinkle with red pepper flakes for a spicy kick.

**Health Benefits:**

- ❖ Quinoa is a complete protein that contains all essential amino acids.
- ❖ Spinach is high in iron and vitamins.
- ❖ This dish is low in salt and potassium, making it ideal for people with CKD.
- ❖ Remember to ask your doctor or a qualified nutritionist for specialized nutritional recommendations.

## 4. Kidney Friendly French Toast

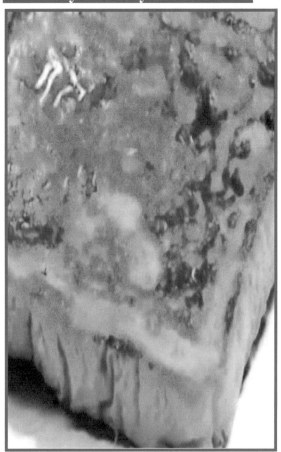

Enjoy a delicious and satisfying meal without jeopardizing your renal health. This kidney-friendly French breakfast recipe is a tasty and nutritious alternative to regular French toast. We produced a tasty breakfast delight by using low-potassium bread and replacing conventional milk with a kidney-friendly alternative.

- ❖ **Preparation time: 5 minutes**
- ❖ **Cooking time: 10 minutes.**
- ❖ **Total time: 15 minutes.**

**Ingredients:**

- ❖ 2 slices of low-potassium bread and 2 large egg whites.

- 1/4 cup low potassium milk (e.g., almond milk)
- 1 teaspoon of vanilla extract.
- 1/4 teaspoon cinnamon.
- Non-stick cooking spray

## Instructions:

- In a small dish, mix together the egg whites, low-potassium milk, vanilla essence, and cinnamon.
- Coat a nonstick skillet with cooking spray and heat over medium heat.
- Dip the bread pieces in the egg mixture, wetting both sides.
- Place the bread in the skillet and heat until both sides are golden brown.
- Serve immediately with your preferred low-potassium toppings, like sugar-free syrup or fresh berries.

### *Serving Size: One serving*

### Nutrition Facts (approximate per serving):

- Calories: 150.
- Carbohydrate: 20g
- Fat: 3g
- Cholesterol: 0 mg.
- Sodium: 50 mg.
- Potassium: 100 mg.
- Phosphorus: 30 mg.
- Protein: 8 grams.
- Fiber: 1 g.

## Cooking Tips:

- To make thicker French toast, soak the bread in egg mixture for a few minutes before cooking.
- Try out several low-potassium milk substitutes, including rice milk or oat milk.
- Serve with a side of fresh fruit for extra nutrients and flavor.

## Health Benefits:

- This recipe is low in potassium and phosphorus, making it suitable for those with CKD.
- Egg whites are a good source of protein without the excessive cholesterol seen in whole eggs.
- Cinnamon may help regulate blood sugar levels.
- Remember to ask your doctor or a qualified nutritionist for specialized nutritional recommendations.

## 5. Low Potassium Smoothie.

This Low Potassium Smoothie is a delightful and nutritious beverage for people with CKD stage 3. This smoothie, which is high in vitamins, minerals, and antioxidants, is a great way to remain hydrated and improve your overall health. With a careful selection of low-potassium ingredients, this recipe makes a tasty and kidney-friendly treat.

- **Preparation time: 5 minutes**
- **Cooking Time: N/A**
- **Total time: 5 minutes.**

### Ingredients:

- 1 cup low potassium fruit (e.g., strawberries, blueberries, or raspberries)
- 1/2 cup low potassium yogurt
- 1/2 cup of low-potassium milk (such almond milk or rice milk)
- 1 tablespoon ground flaxseed.
- 1/4 cup ice cubes.
- Sweetener (optional: stevia or monk fruit)

### Instructions:

- Combine all of the ingredients in a blender.
- Blend until smooth and creamy.
- Use the optional sweetener to adjust the sweetness to your taste.

*Serving Size: One serving*

### Nutrition Facts (approximate per serving):

- Calories: 150.
- Carbohydrate: 25 grams
- Fat: 3g
- Cholesterol: 0 mg.
- Sodium: 50 mg.
- Potassium: 100 mg.
- Phosphorus: 30 mg.
- Protein: 5 grams.
- Fiber: 3 grams.

### Cooking Tips:

- Experiment with low-potassium fruits and vegetables to generate diverse flavors.
- Frozen fruit can be used instead of fresh to increase thickness.
- To increase the protein content, add a scoop of plant-based protein powder.

### Health benefits:

- Promotes hydration.
- Fiber promotes gut health.
- It is low in potassium, making it appropriate for people with chronic kidney disease.
- Remember to ask your doctor or a qualified nutritionist for specialized nutritional recommendations.

## 6. Low-sodium vegetable omelet

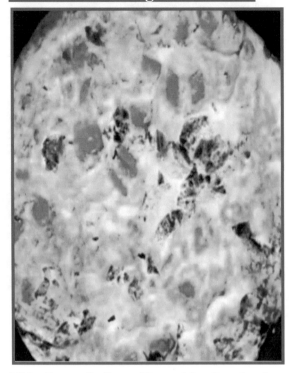

This Low Sodium Vegetable Omelet is a delicious and healthy meal ideal for people with dietary limitations, such as those with CKD. This omelet, which is high in protein and other nutrients, is a great way to enjoy a filling breakfast or lunch while staying under sodium limits. We produced a tasty recipe that is low in salt by carefully selecting components.

- ❖ *Preparation time: 5 minutes*
- ❖ *Cooking time: 10 minutes.*
- ❖ *Total time: 15 minutes.*

### Ingredients:

- ❖ 2 egg whites.
- ❖ 1/4 cup reduced sodium cottage cheese
- ❖ 1/4 cup chopped onion.
- ❖ 1/4 cup diced bell pepper.
- ❖ 1/4 cup chopped spinach.
- ❖ 1 tablespoon of olive oil.
- ❖ Dried herbs (e.g., basil, oregano) to taste.
- ❖ Add black pepper to taste.

### Instructions:

- ❖ In a mixing dish, combine egg whites and cottage cheese and stir until smooth.
- ❖ In a nonstick skillet, heat olive oil over medium heat.
- ❖ Cook the onion and bell pepper in the skillet for about 3 minutes, or until softened.
- ❖ Add the spinach and simmer for about 1 minute, or until wilted.
- ❖ Pour the egg white mixture over the vegetable mixture and scramble for 5 minutes, or until thoroughly cooked.
- ❖ Season with dried herbs and black pepper to taste.

*Serving Size: One serving*

### Nutrition Facts (approximate per serving):

- ❖ Calories: 120.
- ❖ Carbs: 3g
- ❖ Fat: 7g
- ❖ Cholesterol: 0 mg.
- ❖ Sodium: 100 mg.
- ❖ Potassium: 200 mg.
- ❖ Phosphorus: 80 mg.
- ❖ Protein: 12 grams.
- ❖ Fiber: 2 grams.

**Cooking Tips:**

❖ To enhance flavor, add a pinch of garlic or onion powder.
❖ Experiment with other vegetables like mushrooms, tomatoes, and zucchini.
❖ To round up the meal, serve with whole-grain toast.

**Health benefits:**

❖ It is low in salt, making it ideal for people who have dietary limitations.
❖ Vegetables are rich in vitamins and minerals.
❖ The reduced salt concentration promotes heart health.
❖ Remember to ask your doctor or a qualified nutritionist for specialized nutritional recommendations.

## 7. Blueberry oatmeal with almond milk.

This Blueberry Oatmeal with Almond Milk is a filling and nutritious breakfast that is also delicious and heart-healthy. Fiber-rich oats, antioxidant-packed blueberries, and protein-packed almond milk make for a well-balanced breakfast. This recipe is also appropriate for those with dietary restrictions because it is low in cholesterol and sodium.

❖ *Preparation time: 5 minutes*
❖ *Cook time: 5 minutes.*
❖ *Total time: 10 minutes.*

**Ingredients:**

❖ 1/2 cup old-fashioned rolled oats.
❖ 1 cup of unsweetened almond milk.
❖ 1/4 cup blueberries, fresh or frozen.

- ❖ A pinch of salt.
- ❖ Optional toppings include sliced almonds, chia seeds, cinnamon, maple syrup.

## Instructions:

- ❖ In a small saucepan, combine the oatmeal, almond milk, and salt.
- ❖ Bring to a boil, then reduce to a low heat and cook for 5 minutes, or until desired consistency.
- ❖ Stir in the blueberries and simmer for another minute.
- ❖ Pour oats into a bowl and top with your preferred toppings.

*Serving Size: One serving*

**Nutrition Facts (approximate per serving):**

- ❖ Calories: 150.
- ❖ Carbohydrate: 25 grams
- ❖ Fat: 5g
- ❖ Cholesterol: 0 mg.
- ❖ Sodium: 50 mg.
- ❖ Potassium: 150 mg.
- ❖ Phosphorus: 60 mg.
- ❖ Protein: 5 grams.
- ❖ Fiber: 4 grams.

## Cooking Tips:

- ❖ For thicker oatmeal, use less almond milk or cook longer.
- ❖ Sprinkle it with cinnamon or nutmeg to enhance the flavor.
- ❖ For a chilly option, prepare oatmeal the night before and chill. Reheat in the morning.
- ❖ Add Greek yogurt for an extra protein boost.

## Health Benefits:

- ❖ Oats include soluble fiber, which reduces cholesterol and regulates blood sugar.
- ❖ Blueberries are high in antioxidants, which protect cells from harm.
- ❖ Almond milk contains calcium and vitamin E.
- ❖ This recipe is minimal in sodium and cholesterol, therefore it is good for your heart.

## Lunch Recipes

### 1. Lentil And Vegetable Soup

This hearty Lentil and Vegetable Soup is a nutritious and fulfilling meal high in protein, fiber, and important vitamins. This soup is ideal for anyone trying to add more plant-based meals into their diet, as well as those with dietary restrictions, due to its low cholesterol and sodium content.

- ❖ *Preparation time: 15 minutes*
- ❖ *Cook time: 45 minutes.*
- ❖ *Total time: 60 minutes.*

**Ingredients:**

- ❖ 1 cup washed green lentils, 1 big onion, 2 chopped carrots, 2 chopped celery stalks, and 4 minced garlic cloves.
- ❖ 4 cups veggie broth.
- ❖ 1 teaspoon dried thyme.
- ❖ 1/2 teaspoon of dried oregano.
- ❖ 1/4 teaspoon of black pepper.
- ❖ 1/4 cup chopped fresh parsley.
- ❖ Optional: 1/4 cup cooked brown rice (to provide texture).

**Instructions:**

- ❖ In a large pot, sauté the onions, carrots, and celery in olive oil until tender.
- ❖ Cook for one more minute after adding the garlic.
- ❖ Combine the lentils, vegetable broth, thyme, oregano, and black pepper.
- ❖ Bring to a boil, then reduce the heat and simmer for 30-40 minutes, or until the lentils are cooked.
- ❖ Add fresh parsley and cooked brown rice (optional).
- ❖ Season to taste.

*Serving size: one cup.*

**Nutrition Facts (approximate per serving):**

- ❖ Calories: 180
- ❖ Carbohydrate: 25 grams
- ❖ Fat: 3g
- ❖ Cholesterol: 0 mg.
- ❖ Sodium: 150 mg.
- ❖ Potassium: 400 mg.
- ❖ Phosphorus: 120 mg.
- ❖ Protein: 12 grams.
- ❖ Fiber: 6 grams.

**Cooking Tips:**

- ❖ To thicken the soup, mash some lentils with a potato masher.
- ❖ Add additional veggies, such as spinach or kale.
- ❖ To finish the meal, serve with whole grain bread.
- ❖ Refrigerate leftovers in an airtight jar for up to three days.

**Health benefits:**

- ❖ This soup is low in cholesterol and sodium, which makes it good for your heart.
- ❖ Vegetables are rich in vitamins and minerals.
- ❖ The mix of complex carbohydrates and protein provides sustained energy.

## 2. Tuna & Cucumber Wrap

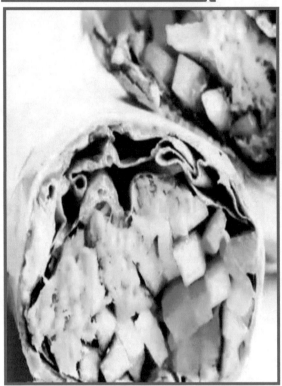

This Tuna and Cucumber Wrap is a light and refreshing meal that is ideal for a quick and nutritious lunch or snack. This wrap, packed with protein from the tuna and important elements from the cucumber, is a delightful and filling meal. This recipe is especially appropriate for individuals limiting their salt consumption because it is a low-sodium supper.

- ❖ Preparation time: 10 minutes
- ❖ Cooking time: N/A
- ❖ Total time: 10 minutes.

**Ingredients:**

- ❖ 1 can (5 ounces) tuna in water, drained
- ❖ 1/4 cup Greek yogurt.
- ❖ 1 tablespoon Dijon mustard.
- ❖ 1/4 teaspoon of dried dill.

- ❖ 1/4 teaspoon of black pepper.
- ❖ 1 large cucumber, thinly sliced
- ❖ 2 whole wheat tortillas.
- ❖ lettuce leaves (optional).

## Instructions:

- ❖ In a mixing bowl, combine tuna, Greek yogurt, Dijon mustard, dill, and black pepper. Mix well.
- ❖ Spread tuna salad equally on one tortilla.
- ❖ Garnish with cucumber slices and lettuce leaves (optional).
- ❖ Wrap firmly and divide in half.

*Serving Size: One wrap.*

## Nutrition Facts (approximate per serving):

- ❖ Calories: 250.
- ❖ Carbohydrate: 25 grams
- ❖ Fat: 10g
- ❖ Cholesterol: 0 mg.
- ❖ Sodium: 150 mg.
- ❖ Potassium: 200 mg.
- ❖ Phosphorus: 100 mg.
- ❖ Protein: 20 grams
- ❖ Fiber: 3 grams.

## Cooking Tips:

- ❖ To enhance the flavor of tuna salad, add chopped red onion or celery.
- ❖ To minimize sodium levels, use low-sodium Greek yogurt.
- ❖ Replace tortillas with lettuce leaves for a low-carb option.
- ❖ Serve with a side salad to complete the meal.

## Health Benefits:

- ❖ Tuna contains lean protein and omega-3 fatty acids.
- ❖ Cucumber is high in water and contains critical vitamins and minerals.
- ❖ Greek yogurt contains protein and probiotics.
- ❖ This wrap is low in sodium and saturated fat, making it a heart-healthy option.

## 3. Chickpea & Spinach Stew

This hearty chickpea and spinach stew is a nutrient-dense meal full of protein, fiber, and minerals. This recipe is ideal on a cold day or as a nutritious lunch alternative. This recipe is also suitable for vegetarians and people who want to minimize their meat consumption.

- ❖ *Preparation time: 15 minutes*
- ❖ *Cook time: 45 minutes.*
- ❖ *Total time: 60 minutes.*

### Ingredients:

- ❖ 1 tablespoon of olive oil.
- ❖ To prepare, chop 1 onion, 2 carrots, 2 celery stalks, and mince 2 cloves of garlic.
- ❖ 1 teaspoon dried thyme.
- ❖ 1/2 teaspoon of dried oregano.
- ❖ 1/4 teaspoon of red pepper flakes.
- ❖ 1 (15 ounce) can of chickpeas, drained and rinsed
- ❖ 4 cups veggie broth.
- ❖ 1 (15-ounce) can of diced tomatoes, undrained
- ❖ 1 cup of fresh spinach, chopped
- ❖ Add salt and pepper to taste.

### Instructions:

- ❖ In a large pot, heat the olive oil over medium heat. Cook the onion, carrots, and celery for about 5 minutes, or until softened.
- ❖ Stir in the garlic, thyme, oregano, and red pepper flakes. Cook for 30 seconds longer.
- ❖ Combine the chickpeas, vegetable broth, and diced tomatoes with their juice. Bring to a boil, then reduce the heat and simmer for 30 minutes.
- ❖ Add the spinach and simmer for about 2 minutes, or until wilted.
- ❖ Season with salt and pepper to taste.

*Serving size: one cup.*

**Nutrition Facts (approximate per serving):**

- ❖ Calories: 200.
- ❖ Carbohydrate: 25 grams
- ❖ Fat: 5g
- ❖ Cholesterol: 0 mg.
- ❖ Sodium: 300 mg.
- ❖ Potassium: 500 mg.
- ❖ Phosphorus: 150 mg.
- ❖ Protein: 10 grams.
- ❖ Fiber: 6 grams.

**Cooking Tips:**

- ❖ To thicken the stew, mash some chickpeas with a potato masher.
- ❖ Add other veggies, such as sweet potatoes or zucchini, for more nutrition.
- ❖ To finish the meal, serve with whole grain bread.
- ❖ Refrigerate leftovers in an airtight jar for up to three days.

**Health Benefits:**

- ❖ Chickpeas are an excellent source of plant-based protein and fiber.
- ❖ This stew is minimal in fat and cholesterol, so it's good for your heart.
- ❖ Vegetables are rich in vitamins and minerals.
- ❖ The mix of complex carbohydrates and protein provides sustained energy.

## 4. Zucchini Noodles with Pesto

Zucchini noodles, or "zoodles," are a low-carb, gluten-free alternative to regular spaghetti. This dish mixes the fresh flavor of zucchini with the rich, savory taste of pesto to create a light and delicious lunch. Ideal for a quick and nutritious entrée or as a side dish.

- ❖ *Preparation time: 15 minutes*
- ❖ *Cook time: 5 minutes.*
- ❖ *Total time: 20 minutes.*

**Ingredients:**

- ❖ 2 huge zucchini.
- ❖ 1/2 cup pesto.
- ❖ 1/4 cup grated parmesan cheese.
- ❖ Add salt and pepper to taste.
- ❖ Optional garnishes include pine nuts and cherry tomatoes.

**Instructions:**

- ❖ Spiralize or peel zucchini to make noodles.
- ❖ In a large bowl, combine the zucchini noodles, pesto, and Parmesan cheese.
- ❖ Toss to coat evenly.
- ❖ Season with salt and pepper to taste.

❖ Serve immediately, with optional pine nuts or cherry tomatoes.

*Serving Size: Two servings*

**Nutrition Facts (approximate per serving):**

❖ Calories: 150.
❖ Carbohydrate: 10 grams
❖ Fat: 10g
❖ Cholesterol: 0 mg.
❖ Sodium: 150 mg.
❖ Potassium: 400 mg.
❖ Phosphorus: 50 mg.
❖ Protein: 5 grams.
❖ Fiber: 3 grams.

**Cooking Tips:**

❖ To enhance taste, sauté zucchini noodles in olive oil before adding pesto.
❖ Experiment with different pestos, including sun-dried tomato or basil pesto.
❖ Add grilled chicken or shrimp for an extra protein boost.
❖ Serve over a bed of spinach for added nutrition.

**Health Benefits:**

❖ Zucchini is a low-calorie vegetable rich in vitamins and minerals.
❖ Pesto contains a high concentration of antioxidants from basil.
❖ This recipe is minimal in carbs and fat, making it a nutritious choice.
❖ An excellent method to enhance your veggie intake.

## 5. Kidney Bean Salad

This Kidney Bean Salad is a filling and nutritious dish full of protein and fiber. This salad is refreshing, savory, and satisfying, making it ideal for a light meal, side dish, or picnic. The mix of kidney beans, veggies, and a tangy dressing results in a tasty and healthful lunch.

❖ *Preparation time: 15 minutes*
❖ *Cooking time: 0 minutes.*
❖ *Total time: 15 minutes.*

**Ingredients:**

❖ 1 can (15 ounces) of kidney beans, rinsed and drained
❖ 1/2 cup diced red onion
❖ 1/2 cup of diced green bell pepper.
❖ 1/4 cup chopped celery.
❖ 1/4 cup chopped fresh parsley.
❖ 1/4 cup olive oil.
❖ 2 tablespoons of red wine vinegar.
❖ 1 tablespoon Dijon mustard.

- ❖ 1 teaspoon honey.
- ❖ Add salt and pepper to taste.

## Instructions:

- ❖ In a large bowl, combine the kidney beans, red onion, green bell pepper, celery, and parsley.
- ❖ In a small bowl, combine the olive oil, red wine vinegar, Dijon mustard, honey, salt, and pepper.
- ❖ Pour the dressing over the bean mixture and toss to coat evenly.
- ❖ Refrigerate for at least 30 minutes before serving to let the flavors combine.

*Serving size: one cup.*

## Nutrition Facts (approximate per serving):

- ❖ Calories: 200.
- ❖ Carbohydrate: 25 grams
- ❖ Fat: 10g
- ❖ Cholesterol: 0 mg.
- ❖ Sodium: 150 mg.
- ❖ Potassium: 400 mg.
- ❖ Phosphorus: 100 mg.
- ❖ Protein: 8 grams.
- ❖ Fiber: 6 grams.

## Cooking Tips:

- ❖ For diversity, try adding corn, cucumber, or tomatoes.
- ❖ To make the salad hotter, add a sprinkle of red pepper flakes to the dressing.
- ❖ Serve over a bed of lettuce for a more substantial supper.
- ❖ Refrigerate leftovers in an airtight jar for up to three days.

## Health Benefits:

- ❖ Kidney beans are an excellent source of plant-based protein and fiber.
- ❖ This salad is low in fat and cholesterol, so it's good for your heart.
- ❖ Vegetables are rich in vitamins and minerals.
- ❖ The mix of complex carbohydrates and protein provides sustained energy.

## 6. Low-sodium turkey sandwich

A low-sodium turkey sandwich is a popular choice for a quick and healthful supper. This recipe focuses on reducing salt while retaining flavor and enjoyment.

- ❖ *Preparation time: 10 minutes*
- ❖ *Cooking Time: N/A*
- ❖ *Total time: 10 minutes.*

### Ingredients:

- ❖ 2 pieces of whole grain bread.
- ❖ 2 ounces. reduced sodium turkey breast
- ❖ 1 tablespoon low-sodium mayonnaise.
- ❖ 1 slice of low-sodium tomato
- ❖ One leaf lettuce
- ❖ Optional: Dijon mustard and red onion.
- ❖ Instructions:
- ❖ Toast the bread to the desired amount of crispiness.
- ❖ Spread low-sodium mayonnaise over one slice of bread.
- ❖ Garnish with turkey breast, tomato, and lettuce.
- ❖ For added taste, mix together a little amount of Dijon mustard and thinly sliced red onion.

- ❖ Cover with the other slice of bread.

*Serving Size: One sandwich.*

### Nutrition Facts (approximate per serving):

- ❖ Calories: 250.
- ❖ Carbs: 30g
- ❖ Fat: 8g
- ❖ Cholesterol: 30 mg.
- ❖ Sodium: 200 mg.
- ❖ Potassium: 250 mg.
- ❖ Phosphorus: 150 mg.
- ❖ Protein: 20 grams
- ❖ Fiber: 3 grams.

### Cooking Tips:

- ❖ Use whole-grain bread for more fiber and nutrients.
- ❖ Experiment with several low-sodium condiments and spreads.
- ❖ Tofu or tempeh can be used instead of turkey as a vegetarian option.

### Health benefits:

- ❖ Avocado slices include healthy fats and potassium.
- ❖ Turkey contains lean protein, which is beneficial for muscle repair and growth.
- ❖ Whole-grain bread contains fiber, which assists digestion and regulates blood sugar.
- ❖ This sandwich is low in sodium, making it ideal for people with high blood pressure.
- ❖ The mix of protein and carbohydrates gives long-lasting energy.

## 7. Grilled Chicken Quinoa Salad

Grilled Chicken Quinoa Salad is a delicious and nutritious dish high in protein, fiber, and healthy fats. The mix of grilled chicken, cooked quinoa, and fresh vegetables results in a tasty and comforting dinner. This salad is ideal for a light lunch or a healthy dinner, and it is an excellent way to add beneficial ingredients into your daily diet.

- ❖ *Preparation time: 20 minutes*
- ❖ *Cook time: 20 minutes.*
- ❖ *Total time: 40 minutes.*

**Ingredients:**

- ❖ 1 cup of quinoa, rinsed
- ❖ 2 cups chicken broth.
- ❖ 2 boneless and skinless chicken breasts.
- ❖ 1/2 cup diced red onion
- ❖ 1/2 cup chopped cucumber.
- ❖ 1/4 cup chopped fresh mint.
- ❖ 1/4 cup olive oil.
- ❖ 2 teaspoons of lemon juice.
- ❖ 1 teaspoon Dijon mustard.
- ❖ Add salt and pepper to taste.

**Instructions:**

- ❖ Cook quinoa: In a medium saucepan, mix the quinoa and chicken broth. Bring to a boil, then reduce heat, cover, and cook for 15 minutes, or until liquid has been absorbed. Fluff with a fork and set aside to cool.
- ❖ Grill chicken: Preheat the grill to medium-high. Season the chicken breasts with salt and pepper. Grill for 8-10 minutes on each side, or until cooked through. Once cooled, cut into cubes.
- ❖ Make the salad: In a large mixing bowl, add cooked quinoa, grilled chicken, red onion, cucumber, and mint.
- ❖ Make a dressing: In a small bowl, combine the olive oil, lemon juice, Dijon mustard, salt, and pepper.
- ❖ Pour dressing over salad and toss to coat evenly.

*Serving Size: One serving*

**Nutrition Facts (approximate per serving):**

- ❖ Calories: 400.
- ❖ Carbs: 30g
- ❖ Fat: 15g
- ❖ Cholesterol: 70 mg.
- ❖ Sodium: 250 mg.

- ❖ Potassium: 400 mg.
- ❖ Phosphorus: 200 mg.
- ❖ Protein: 30 grams.
- ❖ Fiber: 3 grams.

## Cooking Tips:

- ❖ To enhance taste, marinade chicken with olive oil, lemon juice, and herbs before grilling.
- ❖ For more variety, try adding cherry tomatoes, bell peppers, or avocado.
- ❖ Use a pre-cooked quinoa blend for added ease.
- ❖ Refrigerate leftovers in an airtight jar for up to three days.

## Health Benefits:

- ❖ Quinoa is a complete protein that contains all essential amino acids.
- ❖ Grilled chicken is a good source of protein.
- ❖ The veggies and herbs in this salad provide plenty of vitamins, minerals, and antioxidants.
- ❖ The combination of protein, carbs, and healthy fats delivers long-lasting energy.

# Dinner Recipes

## 1. Beef and Vegetable Stir-Fry

This Beef and Vegetable Stir-Fry is a quick and delectable lunch full of protein, vitamins, and minerals. With a focus on fresh ingredients and quick cooking methods, this recipe is both nutritious and enjoyable. The mix of tender meat, vibrant veggies, and a savory sauce results in a delectable and nutritious dinner.

- ❖ *Preparation time: 15 minutes*
- ❖ *Cooking time: 10 minutes.*
- ❖ *Total time: 25 minutes.*

### Ingredients:

- ❖ 1 pound flank steak, thinly sliced.
- ❖ 1 tablespoon of cornstarch.
- ❖ 1 tablespoon of soy sauce (low sodium)
- ❖ 1 tablespoon of oyster sauce (optional).
- ❖ 1/2 teaspoon of garlic powder.
- ❖ 1/4 teaspoon of black pepper.
- ❖ 1 tablespoon of vegetable oil.
- ❖ 1 onion, sliced
- ❖ 1 sliced green bell pepper, 1 sliced carrot, and 1 cup of broccoli florets.
- ❖ 2 garlic cloves, minced
- ❖ 1 tablespoon ginger, minced
- ❖ 1/4 cup of low sodium soy sauce.
- ❖ 1 tablespoon of rice vinegar.
- ❖ 1 teaspoon of sesame oil.

### Instructions:

- ❖ In a bowl, combine the flank steak, cornstarch, soy sauce, oyster sauce, garlic powder, and black pepper. Marinate for ten minutes.
- ❖ Heat the vegetable oil in a big skillet or wok over high heat. Stir-fry the steak until browned and cooked through. Remove from the skillet and set aside.
- ❖ Add the onion, green bell pepper, and carrot to the skillet. Stir-fry for 3-4 minutes, until softened.
- ❖ Stir in the broccoli and cook for two minutes.
- ❖ Stir in the garlic and ginger, and simmer for 30 seconds.
- ❖ Return the beef to the skillet. Combine low-sodium soy sauce, rice vinegar, and sesame oil. Stir until mixed.

*Serving Size: Four servings*

**Nutrition Facts (approximate per serving):**

- ❖ Calories: 350.
- ❖ Carbohydrate: 20g

- ❖ Fat: 15g
- ❖ Cholesterol: 70 mg.
- ❖ Sodium: 400 mg.
- ❖ Potassium: 450 mg.
- ❖ Phosphorus: 150 mg.
- ❖ Protein: 30 grams.
- ❖ Fiber: 4 grams.

## Cooking Tips:

- ❖ To thicken the sauce, add a cornstarch slurry (combined with water) to the skillet and heat until thick.
- ❖ Serve over brown rice or quinoa to complete the meal.
- ❖ Add more veggies, such as snow peas or mushrooms, for variation.
- ❖ To achieve realistic stir-fry results, use a wok.

## Health Benefits:

- ❖ Beef is a good source of lean protein.
- ❖ Vegetables provide important vitamins, minerals, and fiber.
- ❖ This meal has a considerable amount of iron from the beef.
- ❖ Quick cooking procedures help to conserve nutrients.

## 2. Kidney-friendly meatloaf

This kidney-friendly meatloaf is a delicious and filling meal that meets dietary requirements. By carefully selecting low-sodium and low-phosphorus components, we've created a tasty meatloaf that is also nutritional.

- ❖ *Preparation time: 20 minutes*
- ❖ *Cooking time: 50 minutes.*
- ❖ *Total time: 70 minutes.*

## Ingredients:

- ❖ 1 pound lean ground beef (90 percent lean)
- ❖ 1/2 cup bread crumbs.
- ❖ 1/4 cup finely chopped onion.
- ❖ 1 egg
- ❖ 1/4 cup low sodium tomato sauce
- ❖ 1 teaspoon of dried oregano.
- ❖ 1/2 teaspoon of garlic powder.
- ❖ 1/4 teaspoon of black pepper.

**Instructions:**

- ❖ Preheat the oven to 350°F (175°C).
- ❖ In a large mixing bowl, add ground beef, breadcrumbs, onion, egg, tomato sauce, oregano, garlic powder, and black pepper. Mix until thoroughly mixed.
- ❖ Form the mixture into a loaf and place in a loaf pan.
- ❖ Bake for 50 minutes, or until the internal temperature is 160°F (71°C).
- ❖ Allow it cool for several minutes before slicing and serving.

*Serving size: 1/4 of the meatloaf.*

**Nutrition Facts (approximate per serving):**

- ❖ Calories: 250.
- ❖ Carbohydrate: 10 grams
- ❖ Fat: 15g
- ❖ Cholesterol: 70 mg.
- ❖ Sodium: 200 mg.
- ❖ Potassium: 250 mg.
- ❖ Phosphorus: 150 mg.
- ❖ Protein: 25 grams.
- ❖ Fiber: 2 grams.

**Cooking Tips:**

- ❖ To enhance flavor, add a small amount of low-sodium Worcestershire sauce.
- ❖ To round up the dish, serve with roasted vegetables.
- ❖ To decrease fat, drain the meatloaf on a paper towel before serving.
- ❖ Refrigerate leftovers in an airtight jar for up to three days.

**Health Benefits:**

- ❖ Lean ground beef is a good protein source.
- ❖ This recipe is minimal in salt and safe for people with kidney disease.
- ❖ The mix of protein and carbohydrates gives long-lasting energy.
- ❖ Serve with veggies to boost fiber and nutritional intake.

## 3. Roasted turkey breast

Roasted turkey breast is a lean and adaptable protein source that is ideal for a nutritious dinner. This recipe focuses on a basic but tasty preparation that highlights the turkey's natural flavor.

- ❖ *Preparation time: 15 minutes*
- ❖ *Cooking time: 1 hour 30 minutes.*
- ❖ *Total time: 1 hour 45 minutes.*

## Ingredients:

- ❖ 1 boneless, skinless turkey breast (about 3-4 pounds)
- ❖ 1 tablespoon of olive oil.
- ❖ 1 teaspoon dried thyme.
- ❖ 1/2 teaspoon dried rosemary.
- ❖ 1/2 teaspoon of garlic powder.
- ❖ 1/4 teaspoon salt.
- ❖ 1/4 teaspoon of black pepper.

## Instructions:

- ❖ Preheat the oven to 350°F (175°C).
- ❖ In a small bowl, mix together olive oil, thyme, rosemary, garlic powder, salt, and pepper.
- ❖ Apply the olive oil mixture evenly on the turkey breast.
- ❖ Place the turkey breast on a roasting rack inside a baking pan.
- ❖ Roast the turkey in the preheated oven for 1 hour and 30 minutes, or until a meat thermometer inserted into the thickest section registers 165°F (74°C).
- ❖ Remove from the oven and let cool for 10 minutes before carving.

*Serving Size: 3 oz.*

## Nutrition Facts (approximate per serving):

- ❖ Calories: 130.
- ❖ Carbohydrate: 0g
- ❖ Fat: 4g
- ❖ Cholesterol: 70 mg.
- ❖ Sodium: 100 mg.
- ❖ Potassium: 250 mg.
- ❖ Phosphorus: 150 mg.
- ❖ Protein: 25 grams.
- ❖ Fiber: 0 grams.

## Cooking Tips:

- ❖ To enhance taste, fill turkey breasts with herbs or lemon slices before roasting.
- ❖ To keep the turkey moist, baste it with pan juices on occasion.

- ❖ Allow the turkey to rest before carving to retain the juices.
- ❖ Use leftover turkey in sandwiches, salads, and soups.

## Health Benefits:

- ❖ Turkey is a lean protein source that is necessary for muscle growth and repair.
- ❖ It's low in fat and carbohydrates, making it a healthy option.
- ❖ Contains important vitamins and minerals such as niacin and selenium.
- ❖ Versatile protein that may be utilized in a variety of recipes.

## 4. Grilled Tilapia and Mango Salsa

Grilled Tilapia with Mango Salsa is a light and delicious dish ideal for summer. The flaky, grilled tilapia goes perfectly with the sweet and spicy mango salsa. This recipe is full of taste and nutrition, making it a nutritious and filling option.

- ❖ *Preparation time: 20 minutes*
- ❖ *Cooking time: 10 minutes.*
- ❖ *Total time: 30 minutes.*

## Ingredients for tilapia:

- ❖ 4 tilapia filets.
- ❖ 1 tablespoon of olive oil.
- ❖ 1 lime, juiced
- ❖ 1/2 teaspoon of garlic powder.
- ❖ 1/4 teaspoon salt.
- ❖ 1/4 teaspoon of black pepper.

*For the mango salsa:*

- ❖ To prepare, dice 1 ripe mango, 1/2 red bell pepper, and 1/4 finely sliced red onion.
- ❖ 1 tablespoon of fresh lime juice.
- ❖ 1 tablespoon of chopped fresh cilantro.
- ❖ 1/4 teaspoon salt.
- ❖ 1/8 teaspoon of black pepper.

## Instructions:

*For tilapia:*

- ❖ In a small bowl, mix together the olive oil, lime juice, garlic powder, salt, and pepper.
- ❖ Brush the marinade over the tilapia filets on both sides.
- ❖ Preheat the grill to medium-high heat.
- ❖ Grill the tilapia filets for 4-5 minutes on each side, or until cooked through and flaky.

*For the mango salsa:*

- ❖ In a medium mixing bowl, combine mango, red bell pepper, red onion, lime juice, cilantro, salt, and pepper.
- ❖ Stir gently to mix.

*Serving Size: One serving (1 tilapia filet and 1/4 cup salsa).*

**Nutrition Facts (approximate per serving):**

- ❖ Calories: 250.
- ❖ Carbohydrate: 20g
- ❖ Fat: 10g
- ❖ Cholesterol: 70 mg.
- ❖ Sodium: 200 mg.
- ❖ Potassium: 400 mg.
- ❖ Phosphorus: 150 mg.
- ❖ Protein: 30 grams.
- ❖ Fiber: 3 grams.

## Cooking Tips:

- ❖ To enhance taste, marinate tilapia for 15-30 minutes before grilling.
- ❖ To give the mango salsa a fiery touch, add a sprinkle of chili powder.
- ❖ To complete the meal, serve with brown rice or quinoa.
- ❖ Refrigerate leftover salsa in an airtight container for up to three days.

## Healthy Benefits:

- ❖ Tilapia contains lean protein and omega-3 fatty acids, making it a healthy choice.
- ❖ Mango is high in vitamins A, C, and fiber.
- ❖ This recipe has low saturated fat and cholesterol, making it a heart-healthy choice.
- ❖ The combination of protein, carbs, and healthy fats delivers long-lasting energy.

## 5. Lemon Garlic Chicken

Lemon garlic chicken is a traditional recipe that is both simple and delectable. This dish calls for juicy chicken breasts wrapped in a zesty lemon and garlic marinade, which results in a tender and tasty main meal.

- ❖ *Preparation time: 15 minutes*
- ❖ *Cook time: 30 minutes.*
- ❖ *Total time: 45 minutes.*

## Ingredients:

- ❖ 4 boneless and skinless chicken breasts.
- ❖ 1/4 cup olive oil.
- ❖ 2 garlic cloves, minced
- ❖ 1 lemon, zested and squeezed
- ❖ 1 tablespoon of dried oregano.
- ❖ 1 teaspoon dried thyme.
- ❖ 1/2 teaspoon of salt.
- ❖ 1/4 teaspoon of black pepper.

## Instructions:

- ❖ Preheat the oven to 400° F (200° C).
- ❖ In a small mixing bowl, combine olive oil, garlic, lemon zest and juice, oregano, thyme, salt, and pepper.
- ❖ Place the chicken breasts in a zip-top bag or shallow dish, then pour in the marinade. Marinate for at least 15 minutes, and up to an hour for the best taste.
- ❖ Remove the chicken from the marinade and transfer to a baking sheet lined with parchment paper.
- ❖ Bake for 25-30 minutes, or until the chicken is thoroughly cooked and the juices run clear.

*Serving Size: One chicken breast.*

**Nutrition Facts (approximate per serving):**

- ❖ Calories: 250.
- ❖ Carbs: 2g
- ❖ Fat: 12g
- ❖ Cholesterol: 80 mg.
- ❖ Sodium: 150 mg.
- ❖ Potassium: 300 mg.
- ❖ Phosphorus: 150 mg.
- ❖ Protein: 30 grams.
- ❖ Fiber: 1 g.

## Cooking Tips:

- ❖ Cooking tip: Pair with roasted veggies or a side salad for a full dinner.

- ❖ After roasting the chicken, broil it for a few minutes to get the skin crispy.
- ❖ Serve leftover chicken in salads, sandwiches, or soups.
- ❖ For more chicken, double the marinade.

## Health Benefits:

- ❖ Chicken is a lean protein source that helps grow and repair tissues.
- ❖ Lemons and garlic have antioxidant qualities.
- ❖ Olive oil contains healthful fats.
- ❖ This recipe is low in carbohydrates but heavy in protein, making it a filling and healthful option.

## 6. Steamed Vegetables with Brown Rice

This simple but nutritious recipe is an excellent starting point for a balanced supper. The combination of steamed vegetables and whole-grain brown rice balances vitamins, minerals, and fiber. It's a versatile base that can be tweaked with different vegetables and ingredients to your liking.

- ❖ *Preparation time: 10 minutes*
- ❖ *Cook time: 30 minutes.*
- ❖ *Total time: 40 minutes.*

## Ingredients:

- ❖ 1 cup brown rice.
- ❖ 2 glasses of water.
- ❖ 2 cups of mixed veggies (broccoli, carrots, green beans, and bell pepper)
- ❖ Add salt and pepper to taste.

## Instructions:

- ❖ Rinse the brown rice thoroughly with cold water.
- ❖ In a medium saucepan, add brown rice and water. Bring to a boil, then lower to a low heat, cover, and cook for 30 minutes, or until the water has been absorbed and the rice is soft.
- ❖ While the rice is cooking, prepare the vegetables. Wash the vegetables and cut them into bite-size pieces.
- ❖ Heat a kettle of salted water to a boil. Add the vegetables and steam for 5-7 minutes, or until tender and crisp. Drain the vegetables.
- ❖ Serve the boiled vegetables over cooked brown rice. Season with salt and pepper to taste.

### Serving Size: One serving

## Nutrition Facts (approximate per serving):

- ❖ Calories: 300.
- ❖ Carbohydrate: 50 grams
- ❖ Fat: 3g
- ❖ Cholesterol: 0 mg.
- ❖ Sodium: 100 mg.
- ❖ Potassium: 400 mg.
- ❖ Phosphorus: 150 mg.
- ❖ Protein: 8 grams.
- ❖ Fiber: 6 grams.

## Cooking Tips:

- ❖ To enhance taste, sprinkle vegetables with a mild olive oil and lemon juice mixture before steaming.
- ❖ Experiment using different vegetables according to your preferences and seasonal availability.
- ❖ To improve the flavor of the brown rice, add a bay leaf to the cooking water.
- ❖ Serve with grilled chicken or tofu for a complete dinner.

## Health Benefits:

- ❖ Brown rice is a complete grain high in fiber, which improves digestion and increases satiety.
- ❖ Steamed veggies preserve their nutrition, which include important vitamins, minerals, and antioxidants.
- ❖ This recipe has low fat and cholesterol, making it a heart-healthy choice.
- ❖ A versatile foundation for many meal combinations.

## 7. Baked Salmon with Herb Sauce

This dish calls for a tasty and healthful baked salmon topped with a fresh herb sauce. The combination of flaky salmon with bright, floral aromas results in a tasty and gratifying dish.

- ❖ *Preparation time: 15 minutes*
- ❖ *Cook time: 20-25 minutes.*
- ❖ *Total Time: 35-40 minutes.*

**Ingredients:**

*For salmon:*

- ❖ 4 salmon filets (about 6 ounces each)
- ❖ 1 tablespoon of olive oil.
- ❖ 1/2 teaspoon of salt.
- ❖ 1/4 teaspoon of black pepper.

*For Herb Sauce:*

- ❖ 1/2 cup packed fresh parsley, chopped.
- ❖ 1/4 cup packed fresh dill, chopped.
- ❖ 2 teaspoons of lemon juice.

- ❖ 2 garlic cloves, minced
- ❖ 2 tablespoons of olive oil.
- ❖ Add salt and pepper to taste.

**Instructions:**

- ❖ Preheat the oven to 400° F (200° C).
- ❖ In a small bowl, add the olive oil, salt, and pepper. Rub the salmon filets with the mixture.
- ❖ Arrange the salmon filets on a baking pan lined with parchment paper.
- ❖ Bake for 20-25 minutes, or until the salmon is thoroughly cooked and readily flaked with a fork.
- ❖ While the salmon is baking, make the herb sauce by putting all of the ingredients in a small bowl and stirring until thoroughly incorporated.
- ❖ Serve the cooked fish topped with the herb sauce.

*Serving size: one salmon filet with 1/4 cup herb sauce.*

**Nutrition Facts (approximate per serving):**

- ❖ Calories: 250.
- ❖ Carbs: 2g
- ❖ Fat: 12g
- ❖ Cholesterol: 70 mg.
- ❖ Sodium: 150 mg.
- ❖ Potassium: 300 mg.
- ❖ Phosphorus: 150 mg.
- ❖ Protein: 30 grams.
- ❖ Fiber: 1 g.

**Cooking Tips:**

❖ To achieve crispy skin, broil fish after baking for a few minutes.

❖ To round out the dish, serve with roasted veggies or a side salad.

❖ Try various herbs, such as basil or chives, for the herb sauce.

❖ To give the herb sauce a creamier texture, add a dollop of Greek yogurt.

**Health Benefits:**

❖ Salmon contains omega-3 fatty acids, which promote heart health.

❖ The mix of protein and healthy fats delivers long-lasting energy.

❖ Herbs and lemon juice enhance the dish while also providing antioxidants.

❖ This meal is low in carbohydrates but heavy in protein, making it a filling and nutritious option.

# Chapter 3

## Mouth Watering Snack and Dessert Recipes

### 1. Baked kale chips

Baked kale chips are a nutritious, crunchy snack. This easy dish turns rough kale leaves into a crispy and pleasant snack. These kale chips are the ideal guilt-free snack because they require few ingredients and are simple to make.

- ❖ *Preparation time: 10 minutes*
- ❖ *Cook time: 15-20 minutes.*
- ❖ *Total Time: 25-30 minutes.*

## Ingredients:

- ❖ 1 bunch of kale
- ❖ 1 tablespoon of olive oil.
- ❖ 1/2 teaspoon salt (to taste)
- ❖ Optional seasonings: garlic powder, onion powder, and red pepper flakes.

## Instructions:

- ❖ Preheat the oven to 350°F (175°C). Line a large baking sheet with parchment paper.
- ❖ Remove and discard the rough stems from the kale leaves. Tear the kale leaves into bite-size pieces.
- ❖ Wash the kale thoroughly and pat it dry using paper towels.
- ❖ In a large bowl, combine the kale, olive oil, and salt. You can also add your desired seasonings at this point.
- ❖ Spread the kale evenly on the prepared baking sheet, making sure no pieces overlap.
- ❖ Bake for 15-20 minutes, or until the kale turns crispy and golden brown. Keep a tight watch on the kale, which may burn rapidly.
- ❖ Allow the kale chips to thoroughly cool on the baking pan before serving.

*Serving size: one cup.*

## Nutrition Facts (approximate per serving):

- ❖ Calories: 80.
- ❖ Carbohydrate: 10 grams
- ❖ Fat: 5g
- ❖ Cholesterol: 0 mg.
- ❖ Sodium: 100 mg.
- ❖ Potassium: 200 mg.
- ❖ Phosphorus: 30 mg.
- ❖ Protein: 2 grams.
- ❖ Fiber: 2 grams.

**Cooking Tips:**

- ❖ Add flavor with ingredients such as Parmesan cheese, nutritional yeast, or chili powder.
- ❖ Do not overcrowd the baking pan so that the kale chips crisp up evenly.
- ❖ If the kale isn't crispy enough after the first roasting time, return it to the oven for a few minutes.
- ❖ Keep leftover kale chips in an airtight container at room temperature.

**Health Benefits:**

- ❖ Kale is loaded with vitamins, minerals, and antioxidants.
- ❖ Kale chips are a low-calorie, low-fat snack choice.
- ❖ This recipe is an excellent way to include more leafy greens to your diet.

## 2. Kidney-Friendly Banana Bread

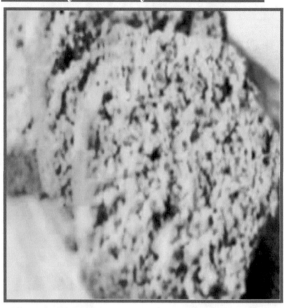

This kidney-friendly banana bread is a tasty and pleasant dessert that meets dietary restrictions. We made a delectable and nutritious banana bread by carefully selecting low-potassium and phosphorus ingredients.

- ❖ *Preparation time: 20 minutes*
- ❖ *Cook time: 50-60 minutes.*
- ❖ *Total Time: 70-80 minutes.*

**Ingredients:**

- ❖ 3 ripe, mashed bananas
- ❖ 1/3 cup unsweetened applesauce.
- ❖ 1/4 cup maple syrup.
- ❖ 1/4 cup vegetable oil.
- ❖ 1 egg white.
- ❖ 1 teaspoon of vanilla extract.
- ❖ 1 cup whole wheat flour.
- ❖ 1/2 cup oat flour.
- ❖ 1 teaspoon of baking powder.
- ❖ 1/2 teaspoon of baking soda.
- ❖ 1/4 teaspoon salt.
- ❖ 1/4 teaspoon cinnamon.

## Instructions:

- ❖ Preheat the oven to 350°F (175°C). Grease and flour the loaf pan.
- ❖ In a large mixing bowl, add mashed bananas, applesauce, maple syrup, vegetable oil, egg whites, and vanilla essence.
- ❖ In a separate bowl, combine the whole wheat flour, oat flour, baking powder, soda, salt, and cinnamon.
- ❖ Gradually combine the dry and wet ingredients, stirring until just blended. Take care not to overmix.
- ❖ Pour the batter into the prepared loaf pan.
- ❖ Bake for 50–60 minutes, or until a toothpick inserted in the center comes out clean.
- ❖ Let cool in the pan for 10 minutes before transferring to a wire rack to finish cooling.

*Serving Size: One slice.*

## Nutrition Facts (approximate per serving):

- ❖ Calories: 150.
- ❖ Carbohydrate: 25 grams
- ❖ Fat: 5g
- ❖ Cholesterol: 0 mg.
- ❖ Sodium: 100 mg.
- ❖ Potassium: 200 mg.
- ❖ Phosphorus: 50 mg.
- ❖ Protein: 3 grams.
- ❖ Fiber: 3 grams.

## Cooking Tips:

- ❖ For a sweeter bread, add more maple syrup.
- ❖ Optional: Add nuts or chocolate chips for added taste and texture.
- ❖ To improve the flavor, use ripe bananas with brown patches.
- ❖ Keep the banana bread in an airtight jar at room temperature for up to three days.

## Health Benefits:

- ❖ Bananas are high in potassium, yet this dish is kidney-friendly.
- ❖ Whole wheat flour contains fiber, which promotes digestive health.
- ❖ This recipe is lower in salt and phosphorus than classic banana bread.
- ❖ Consume in moderation as part of a balanced diet.

## 3. Berry Compote with Greek Yogurt

This light and healthful dessert blends the sweetness of fresh berries and the tangy creaminess of Greek yogurt. The berry compote is quick and easy to create, making it ideal for a light and filling snack.

- ❖ *Preparation time: 10 minutes*
- ❖ *Cooking Time: 5–7 minutes*
- ❖ *Total time: 15–17 minutes*

### Ingredients:

- ❖ 1 cup mixed berries (including strawberries, blueberries, and raspberries)
- ❖ 1 tablespoon sugar (to taste)
- ❖ 1 tablespoon of lemon juice.
- ❖ 1 cup Greek yogurt.
- ❖ Optional garnishes include granola and fresh mint.

### Instructions:

- ❖ In a small saucepan, stir together the mixed berries, sugar, and lemon juice.
- ❖ Bring the mixture to a simmer over medium heat. Reduce the heat and cook for 5-7 minutes, or until the berries have softened and released their juices.
- ❖ Allow the compote to cool slightly before serving.
- ❖ Serve the berry compote over Greek yogurt, topped with granola or fresh mint if desired.

### Serving Size: One serving

### Nutrition Facts (approximate per serving):

- ❖ Calories: 150.
- ❖ Carbohydrate: 20g
- ❖ Fat: 5g
- ❖ Cholesterol: 0 mg.
- ❖ Sodium: 50 mg.
- ❖ Potassium: 300 mg.
- ❖ Phosphorus: 80 mg.
- ❖ Protein: 6 grams.
- ❖ Fiber: 2 grams.

### Cooking Tips:

- ❖ To get a thicker compote, simmer the berries longer.
- ❖ For added flavor, add a pinch of cinnamon or some vanilla extract.
- ❖ If fresh berries are unavailable, use frozen berries instead.
- ❖ For a delightful dessert, serve the compote with pancakes, waffles, or ice cream.

### Health Benefits:

- ❖ Berries provide antioxidants, vitamins, and fiber.
- ❖ Greek yogurt is a good source of protein and calcium.
- ❖ This dessert is minimal in fat and calories, so it's a healthy treat.

## 4. Rice Cakes and Almond Butter

Rice cakes covered with almond butter are a simple but tasty snack that contains a combination of carbohydrates, protein, and healthy fats. This combo gives long-lasting energy and critical nutrients.

- ❖ *Preparation Time: Two minutes*
- ❖ *Cooking Time: N/A*
- ❖ *Total time: two minutes.*

### Ingredients:

- ❖ 1 rice cake.
- ❖ 1 tablespoon almond butter.
- ❖ Optional ingredients: sliced banana, chia seeds, or cinnamon.

### Instructions:

- ❖ Place one rice cake on a platter.
- ❖ Spread almond butter evenly across the top of the rice cake.
- ❖ For added taste and texture, try topping with sliced banana, chia seeds, or cinnamon.

*Serving Size: One serving*

**Nutrition Facts (approximate per serving):**

- ❖ Calories: 170.
- ❖ Carbohydrate: 20g
- ❖ Fat: 12g
- ❖ Cholesterol: 0 mg.
- ❖ Sodium: 100 mg.
- ❖ Potassium: 200 mg.
- ❖ Phosphorus: 100 mg.
- ❖ Protein: 4 grams.
- ❖ Fiber: 2 grams.

### Cooking Tips:

- ❖ Experiment with various nut butters, such as peanut or cashew butter.
- ❖ For extra sweetness, sprinkle with honey or maple syrup.
- ❖ Garnish with fresh fruit slices for extra vitamins and antioxidants.
- ❖ To achieve a crunchier texture, toast the rice cake before adding the almond butter.

### Health Benefits:

- ❖ This snack provides a balanced macronutrient profile for long-lasting energy.
- ❖ The mix of carbohydrates and protein can assist to control blood sugar levels.

## 5. Cottage Cheese with Pineapple

This traditional combination of cottage cheese and pineapple is a delicious and healthful snack or light dinner. The tangy cottage cheese compliments the sweet and juicy pineapple nicely, resulting in a balanced and delicious flavor.

- ❖ *Preparation time: 5 minutes*
- ❖ *Cooking Time: N/A*
- ❖ *Total time: 5 minutes.*

### Ingredients:

- ❖ 1/2 cup low-fat cottage cheese.
- ❖ 1/4 cup diced pineapple.
- ❖ Optional: 1 tablespoon granola and 1 teaspoon chia seeds.

### Instructions:

- ❖ In a bowl, combine the cottage cheese and cubed pineapple.
- ❖ Stir gently to mix.
- ❖ Optional: Add granola and chia seeds for texture and flavor.

*Serving Size: One serving*

**Nutrition Facts (approximate per serving):**

- ❖ Calories: 120.
- ❖ Carbohydrate: 10 grams
- ❖ Fat: 4g
- ❖ Cholesterol: 5 mg.
- ❖ Sodium: 100 mg.
- ❖ Potassium: 250 mg.
- ❖ Phosphorus: 80 mg.
- ❖ Protein: 10 grams.
- ❖ Fiber: 1 g.

### Cooking Tips:

- ❖ For a sweeter flavor, sprinkle with honey or maple syrup.
- ❖ Use fresh pineapple for the best flavor.
- ❖ Experiment with different fruits, such as strawberries or mango.
- ❖ To add extra warmth, sprinkle it with cinnamon or nutmeg.

### Health Benefits:

- ❖ Pineapple contains vitamin C and antioxidants.
- ❖ This snack is minimal in calories and fat, therefore it is a healthy option.

## 6. Low Sodium Hummus with Vegetable Sticks

This low-sodium hummus recipe produces a nutritious and tasty dip high in protein and fiber. This hummus is ideal for a filling snack or appetizer and is served with fresh vegetable sticks for a crunchy and nutritious combo.

- ❖ *Preparation time: 15 minutes*
- ❖ *Cooking Time: N/A*
- ❖ *Total time: 15 minutes.*

### Ingredients:

- ❖ 1 can (15 ounces) of chickpeas, rinsed and drained
- ❖ Three tablespoons of extra-virgin olive oil
- ❖ 2 garlic cloves, minced
- ❖ 1/4 cup of fresh lemon juice.
- ❖ 2 tablespoons tahini.
- ❖ 1/2 teaspoon of ground cumin
- ❖ 1/4 teaspoon paprika.
- ❖ Salt-free herbs (such as dried parsley and dill)
- ❖ Various fresh vegetables (carrots, celery, cucumber, bell pepper) for dipping.

### Instructions:

- ❖ Put the chickpeas, olive oil, garlic, lemon juice, tahini, cumin, paprika, and herbs in a food processor.
- ❖ Process until smooth and creamy, scraping down the sides as necessary.
- ❖ Taste and adjust seasonings as needed.
- ❖ Serve hummus with a selection of fresh veggie sticks.

*Serving size: 1/4 cup hummus and vegetable sticks.*

### Nutrition Facts (approximate per serving):

- ❖ Calories: 150.
- ❖ Carbohydrate: 12g
- ❖ Fat: 10g
- ❖ Cholesterol: 0 mg.
- ❖ Sodium: 50 mg.
- ❖ Potassium: 300 mg.
- ❖ Phosphorus: 100 mg.
- ❖ Protein: 4 grams.
- ❖ Fiber: 4 grams.

**Cooking Tips:**

❖ To get a smoother hummus, add a tablespoon of water during processing.

❖ Experiment with various herbs and spices to add flavor.

❖ Before cooking hummus, roast the chickpeas to provide a smokey taste.

❖ Serve with whole-grain pita or crackers for a more substantial snack.

**Health Benefits:**

❖ Chickpeas contain plant-based protein and fiber.

❖ Hummus is low in both saturated fat and cholesterol.

❖ Vegetable sticks contain vital vitamins, minerals, and fiber.

❖ This snack is both heart-healthy and satisfying.

## 7. Apple Slices with Peanut Butter

Apple slices and peanut butter are a classic combo that makes for a simple but nutritious snack. This combination provides a balanced intake of carbohydrates, protein, and healthy fats to power your body.

❖ **Preparation time: 5 minutes**
❖ **Cooking Time: N/A**
❖ **Total time: 5 minutes.**

**Ingredients:**

❖ 1 medium apple, cleaned and cut.
❖ 2 tablespoons peanut butter.
❖ Optional: cinnamon.
❖ Instructions:
❖ Wash and slice the apples to the appropriate thickness.
❖ Spread a liberal amount of peanut butter onto each apple slice.
❖ Sprinkle with cinnamon if desired.

*Serving Size: 1 serving (1 apple and 2 tbsp peanut butter).*

**Nutrition Facts (approximate per serving):**

- ❖ Calories: 180
- ❖ Carbohydrate: 20g
- ❖ Fat: 12g
- ❖ Cholesterol: 0 mg.
- ❖ Sodium: 100 mg.
- ❖ Potassium: 200 mg.
- ❖ Phosphorus: 100 mg.
- ❖ Protein: 7 grams.
- ❖ Fiber: 3 grams.

**Cooking Tips:**

- ❖ Drizzle honey over apple slices for additional sweetness.
- ❖ Use crunchy peanut butter for added texture.
- ❖ Experiment with various apple kinds to create distinct flavors.
- ❖ Sprinkle chia seeds for added nutrition.

**Health benefits:**

- ❖ Apples contain fiber and vitamin C.
- ❖ Peanut butter contains protein and healthy fats.
- ❖ This snack contains a balanced amount of carbohydrates, protein, and fat for long-lasting energy.
- ❖ The combination may help manage blood sugar levels.

## Soups and Stews Recipes

### 1. Creamy Broccoli Soup

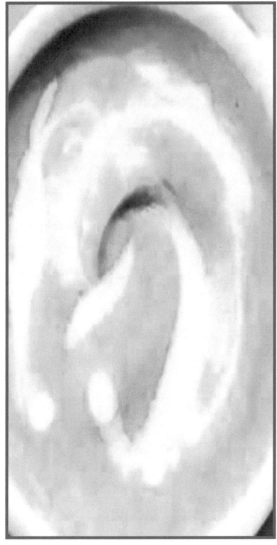

Creamy broccoli soup is a hearty and nutritious recipe ideal for a comfortable meal.

This soup is a delightful way to get your daily dosage of vegetables while still being high in vitamins and minerals.

- ❖ *Preparation time: 15 minutes*
- ❖ *Cook time: 25 minutes.*
- ❖ *Total time: 40 minutes.*

### Ingredients:

- ❖ 1 tablespoon of olive oil.
- ❖ 1 onion, chopped
- ❖ 2 garlic cloves, minced
- ❖ 4 cups chicken broth.
- ❖ 1 head of broccoli, chopped
- ❖ 1/2 cup milk.
- ❖ 1/4 cup all-purpose flour.
- ❖ Add salt and pepper to taste.

### Instructions:

- ❖ In a large pot, heat the olive oil over medium heat. Add the onion and garlic and heat until softened.
- ❖ Stir in the chicken broth and broccoli. Bring to a boil, then reduce the heat and simmer until the broccoli is soft.
- ❖ Use an immersion blender to purée the soup, or transfer it to a blender.
- ❖ In a small saucepan, mix together the milk and flour until smooth. Slowly whisk the milk mixture into the soup, stirring frequently.
- ❖ Return the soup to a simmer and cook until thickened, stirring periodically.
- ❖ Season with salt and pepper to taste.

*Serving size: one cup.*

### Nutrition Facts (approximate per serving):

- ❖ Calories: 150.
- ❖ Carbohydrate: 15 grams
- ❖ Fat: 5g
- ❖ Cholesterol: 10 mg.

- ❖ Sodium: 300 mg.
- ❖ Potassium: 500 mg.
- ❖ Phosphorus: 100 mg.
- ❖ Protein: 5 grams.
- ❖ Fiber: 4 grams.

## Cooking Tips:

- ❖ Use full milk rather than low-fat milk to make the soup creamier.
- ❖ For a deeper flavor, mix in a handful of shredded cheddar cheese.
- ❖ Serve with fresh bread to dip.
- ❖ For a vegan option, use vegetable broth and a plant-based milk substitute.

## Health Benefits:

- ❖ Broccoli is loaded with vitamins, minerals, and antioxidants.
- ❖ This soup contains plenty of fiber and protein.
- ❖ It is a comfortable and filling meal option.

## 2. Lentil and Carrot Soup

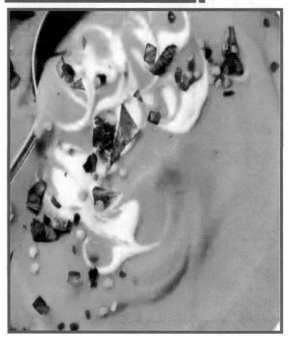

Lentil and carrot soup is a substantial and nutritious dish high in protein and fiber.

This warm soup is ideal for a cold day or a light dinner. The mix of lentils and carrots provides a tasty and pleasant foundation for this nutritious soup.

- ❖ *Preparation time: 15 minutes*
- ❖ *Cook time: 30 minutes.*
- ❖ *Total time: 45 minutes.*

## Ingredients:

- ❖ 1 tablespoon of olive oil.
- ❖ 1 onion, chopped
- ❖ Two carrots, chopped.
- ❖ 2 garlic cloves, minced
- ❖ 1 cup green lentils, washed
- ❖ 4 cups veggie broth.
- ❖ 1 bay leaf.
- ❖ Add salt and pepper to taste.

❖ Fresh parsley for garnish (optional)

**Instructions:**

❖ In a large pot, heat the olive oil over medium heat. Add the onion and simmer until softened.
❖ Cook for an additional 2 minutes after stirring in the carrots and garlic.
❖ Add the lentils, vegetable broth, and bay leaf to the pot. Bring to a boil, then reduce the heat and simmer for 30 minutes, or until the lentils are cooked.
❖ Remove the bay leaf. Season with salt and pepper to taste.
❖ Serve hot, topped with fresh parsley if preferred.

*Serving size: one cup.*

**Nutrition Facts (approximate per serving):**

❖ Calories: 150.
❖ Carbohydrate: 20g
❖ Fat: 3g
❖ Cholesterol: 0 mg.
❖ Sodium: 200 mg.
❖ Potassium: 400 mg.
❖ Phosphorus: 100 mg.
❖ Protein: 8 grams.
❖ Fiber: 6 grams.

**Cooking Tips:**

❖ To make the soup creamier, purée a portion of it with an immersion blender or blender before returning it to the saucepan.
❖ For added taste and minerals, include other veggies like celery or sweet potatoes.
❖ Serve with fresh bread to dip.
❖ Sauté some chopped pancetta or bacon before adding the onion to get a deeper flavor.

**Health Benefits:**

❖ Lentils are an excellent source of plant-based protein and fiber.
❖ Carrots contain vitamins, minerals, and antioxidants.
❖ This soup is low in fat and cholesterol, making it a heart-healthy choice.
❖ It's a full and fulfilling supper that promotes overall wellness.

## 3. Beef & Barley Stew

Beef and barley stew is a traditional comfort food that is both filling and nourishing. This stew is packed with protein and fiber, making it an excellent choice for a cold day. The mix of tender meat, fragrant broth, and chewy barley results in a tasty and nutritious dinner.

- ❖ *Preparation time: 30 minutes*
- ❖ *Cooking time: two hours.*
- ❖ *Total time: 2 hours 30 minutes.*

## Ingredients:

- ❖ 1 pound beef chuck, cut into 1 inch cubes.
- ❖ 1 tablespoon of olive oil.
- ❖ 1 onion, chopped
- ❖ 2 carrots, chopped.
- ❖ 2 celery stalks, chopped
- ❖ 4 garlic cloves, minced
- ❖ 1 tablespoon of Worcestershire sauce.
- ❖ 1 teaspoon dried thyme.
- ❖ 1/2 teaspoon of black pepper.
- ❖ 4 cups of beef broth.
- ❖ 1 cup pearl barley, washed.
- ❖ 1 bay leaf.
- ❖ Salt to taste.

## Instructions:

- ❖ In a large Dutch oven, heat the olive oil on medium-high. Brown the beef on all sides. Remove the steak from the saucepan and set it aside.
- ❖ Add the onions, carrots, and celery to the pot. Cook for approximately 5 minutes, or until softened. Stir in the garlic and heat for another 30 seconds.
- ❖ Return the steak to the boil and season with Worcestershire sauce, thyme, and black pepper. Stir to mix.
- ❖ Pour in the beef stock and bring to a boil. Reduce the heat, cover, and simmer for 1 hour.
- ❖ Add the barley and bay leaf to the saucepan. Continue to simmer for another hour, or until the beef is soft and the barley is fully cooked.
- ❖ Remove the bay leaf before serving. Season with salt to taste.

*Serving size: one cup.*

**Nutrition Facts (approximate per serving):**

- ❖ Calories: 250.
- ❖ Carbohydrate: 25 grams
- ❖ Fat: 10g
- ❖ Cholesterol: 70 mg.
- ❖ Sodium: 400 mg.
- ❖ Potassium: 450 mg.

- ❖ Phosphorus: 150 mg.
- ❖ Protein: 20 grams
- ❖ Fiber: 5 grams.

**Cooking Tips:**

- ❖ To make a thicker stew, purée some of the soup with an immersion blender before returning it to the saucepan.
- ❖ Add other veggies, like potatoes or parsnips, to boost taste and nutrition.
- ❖ Serve with fresh bread to dip.
- ❖ Refrigerate leftovers in an airtight jar for up to three days.

**Health Benefits:**

- ❖ Beef is an excellent source of protein and iron.
- ❖ Barley is a whole grain high in fiber.
- ❖ This stew is a hearty and fulfilling meal that gives long-lasting energy.
- ❖ The combination of protein, carbohydrates, and veggies makes it a well-balanced meal.

## 4. Chicken & Rice Soup

Chicken and rice soup is a traditional comfort food that is both nutritious and enjoyable. This substantial soup has protein, carbs, and necessary elements, making it an ideal supper for a cold day.

- ❖ *Preparation time: 15 minutes*
- ❖ *Cook time: 45 minutes.*
- ❖ *Total time: 60 minutes.*

**Ingredients:**

- ❖ 1 tablespoon of olive oil.
- ❖ 1 onion, chopped
- ❖ 2 carrots, chopped.
- ❖ 2 celery stalks, chopped
- ❖ 2 garlic cloves, minced
- ❖ 1 pound of boneless, skinless chicken breasts.
- ❖ 8 cups chicken broth.
- ❖ 1 cup white rice.
- ❖ 1/2 teaspoon dried thyme.

- ❖ 1/4 teaspoon of black pepper.
- ❖ Salt to taste.

## Instructions:

- ❖ In a large pot, heat the olive oil over medium heat. Add the onion, carrots, and celery and simmer until tender. Stir in the garlic and heat for another 30 seconds.
- ❖ Add the chicken breasts, stock, and thyme to the pot. Bring to a boil, then reduce heat and simmer for 20 minutes, or until the chicken is fully cooked.
- ❖ Remove the chicken from the saucepan and shred.
- ❖ Add rice and black pepper to the soup. Bring to a boil, then reduce heat, cover, and simmer for 20 minutes, or until rice is fully cooked.
- ❖ Return the shredded chicken to the broth and season with salt to taste.

*Serving size: one cup.*

## Nutrition Facts (approximate per serving):

- ❖ Calories: 250.
- ❖ Carbs: 30g
- ❖ Fat: 5g
- ❖ Cholesterol: 70 mg.
- ❖ Sodium: 400 mg.
- ❖ Potassium: 450 mg.
- ❖ Phosphorus: 150 mg.
- ❖ Protein: 25 grams.
- ❖ Fiber: 1 g.

## Cooking Tips:

- ❖ Cook the rice until it has absorbed the majority of the liquid to make the soup thicker.
- ❖ Add additional veggies, such as peas or corn, for added nutrition.
- ❖ Serve with fresh bread to dip.
- ❖ Roast the chicken before shredding it to get a deeper taste.

## Health Benefits:

- ❖ Chicken is an excellent source of lean protein.
- ❖ Rice supplies carbs for energy.
- ❖ This soup is a hearty and filling supper that is low in fat.
- ❖ It is a well-balanced meal because it contains both protein and carbohydrates.

## 5. Hearty Vegetable Soup

This hearty vegetable soup is a nutritious and filling supper. This soup, packed with vegetables, is a delightful way to integrate more plant-based meals into your diet. It's a satisfying and nutritious option for any occasion.

- *Preparation time: 15 minutes*
- *Cook time: 45 minutes.*
- *Total time: 60 minutes.*

**Ingredients:**

- 1 tablespoon of olive oil.
- 1 onion, chopped
- 2 carrots, chopped.
- 2 celery stalks, chopped
- 2 garlic cloves, minced
- 4 cups veggie broth.
- 1 big potato, diced
- 1 cup frozen corn.
- 1 cup frozen peas.
- 1 can (15 ounces) of chickpeas, drained and rinsed
- 1 bay leaf.
- Add salt and pepper to taste.
- Fresh parsley for garnish (optional)

**Instructions:**

- In a large pot, heat the olive oil over medium heat. Sauté the onion, carrots, and celery until tender. Cook for a further 30 seconds after adding the garlic.
- Stir in the vegetable broth, potato, corn, peas, chickpeas, and bay leaf. Bring to a boil, then reduce the heat and simmer for 30 minutes, or until the veggies are soft.
- Remove the bay leaf. Season with salt and pepper to taste.
- Serve hot, topped with fresh parsley if preferred.

**Serving size: one cup.**

**Nutrition Facts (approximate per serving):**

- Calories: 150.
- Carbohydrate: 20g
- Fat: 5g
- Cholesterol: 0 mg.
- Sodium: 300 mg.
- Potassium: 600 mg.
- Phosphorus: 150 mg.
- Protein: 7 grams.
- Fiber: 6 grams.

**Cooking Tips:**

❖ To make a thicker soup, purée a portion of it with an immersion blender before returning it to the saucepan.

❖ Add other veggies, such as zucchini, green beans, or spinach for variation.

❖ Serve with fresh bread to dip.

❖ To give the soup a deeper taste, add a teaspoon of curry powder or cumin.

**Health Benefits:**

❖ The diversity of veggies in this soup provide plenty of vitamins, minerals, and fiber.

❖ It is a low-calorie, low-fat meal choice.

❖ Chickpeas include plant-based protein.

❖ This rich and comforting soup promotes general health and well-being.

# Chapter 4

## Smoothies & Drinks Recipes

### 1. Tropical Pineapple Smoothie

This tropical pineapple smoothie is both delicious and nutritious, filled with vitamins and antioxidants. It's the ideal way to start the day or get a healthy boost. The sweetness of the pineapple, mixed with the creamy texture, results in a tasty and gratifying dessert.

- ❖ *Preparation time: 5 minutes*
- ❖ *Cooking Time: N/A*
- ❖ *Total time: 5 minutes.*

### Ingredients:

- ❖ 1 cup pineapple chunks (fresh or frozen)
- ❖ 1/2 banana, cut.
- ❖ 1/2 cup unsweetened coconut milk.
- ❖ 1/4 cup plain Greek yogurt.
- ❖ 1/4 cup orange juice.
- ❖ Optional toppings include 1 tablespoon chia seeds, honey, or coconut flakes.
- ❖ Instructions:
- ❖ Combine all of the ingredients in a blender.
- ❖ Blend until smooth and creamy.

- ❖ Pour into a glass and drink immediately.

*Serving Size: One serving*

### Nutrition Facts (approximate per serving):

- ❖ Calories: 150.
- ❖ Carbohydrate: 25 grams
- ❖ Fat: 5g
- ❖ Cholesterol: 0 mg.
- ❖ Sodium: 30 mg.
- ❖ Potassium: 400 mg.
- ❖ Phosphorus: 80 mg.
- ❖ Protein: 5 grams.
- ❖ Fiber: 3 grams.

### Cooking Tips:

- ❖ To make a thicker smoothie, use frozen pineapple or a handful of ice cubes.
- ❖ Experiment with various fruit and yogurt flavors.
- ❖ Add a scoop of protein powder to make the smoothie more filling.
- ❖ Garnish with a pineapple slice or a sprinkle of coconut flakes to finish.

### Health Benefits:

- ❖ Pineapples are high in vitamin C and antioxidants.
- ❖ Greek yogurt contains protein and calcium.
- ❖ Coconut milk provides healthful fats and flavor.
- ❖ This smoothie is both refreshing and hydrating.

## 2. Apple-Ginger Smoothie

This delightful Apple Ginger Smoothie is the ideal way to start the day or for a nutritious pick-me-up. The mix of sweet apples and spicy ginger produces a tasty and energizing beverage.

This smoothie is a nutritious choice for any time of day, thanks to its high vitamin and antioxidant content.

- ❖ *Preparation time: 5 minutes*
- ❖ *Cooking Time: N/A*
- ❖ *Total time: 5 minutes.*

### Ingredients:

- ❖ One large apple, cored and cut.
- ❖ 1 inch of ginger, peeled and grated.
- ❖ 1 cup of unsweetened almond milk.
- ❖ 1/4 cup of plain Greek yogurt (optional)
- ❖ One teaspoon honey (optional)
- ❖ Ice cubes
- ❖ Instructions:
- ❖ In a blender, combine apple, ginger, almond milk, Greek yogurt, and honey (if desired).
- ❖ Blend until smooth and creamy.

- ❖ Add ice cubes and blend again until the desired consistency is achieved.

*Serving Size: One serving*

**Nutrition Facts (approximate per serving):**

- ❖ Calories: 150.
- ❖ Carbohydrate: 25 grams
- ❖ Fat: 5g
- ❖ Cholesterol: 0 mg.
- ❖ Sodium: 30 mg.
- ❖ Potassium: 400 mg.
- ❖ Phosphorus: 80 mg.
- ❖ Protein: 5 grams.
- ❖ Fiber: 3 grams.

### Cooking Tips:

- ❖ To make the smoothie sweeter, add a ripe banana or a date.
- ❖ Use frozen apple slices to achieve a thicker consistency.
- ❖ Experiment with different kinds of milk, including soy or oat milk.
- ❖ Sprinkle it with cinnamon or nutmeg for extra taste.

### Health Benefits:

- ❖ Apples are rich in fiber and vitamin C.
- ❖ Ginger contains anti-inflammatory effects and can assist digestion.
- ❖ Greek yogurt contains protein and calcium.
- ❖ This smoothie is both refreshing and hydrating.

## 3. Strawberry Banana Smoothie

The Strawberry Banana Smoothie, a traditional combo, is both pleasant and nourishing.

This smoothie, which is high in vitamins, minerals, and antioxidants, is ideal for starting the day or as a healthy snack.

- ❖ *Preparation time: 5 minutes*
- ❖ *Cooking Time: N/A*
- ❖ *Total time: 5 minutes.*

### Ingredients:

- ❖ 1 cup strawberries, fresh or frozen.
- ❖ One ripe banana, cut
- ❖ 1 cup of unsweetened almond milk (or your chosen milk).
- ❖ 1/4 cup of plain Greek yogurt (optional)
- ❖ 1 teaspoon honey (optional)
- ❖ Ice cubes

### Instructions:

- ❖ In a blender, combine strawberries, banana, almond milk, Greek yogurt, and honey (optional).
- ❖ Blend until smooth and creamy.
- ❖ Add ice cubes and blend again until the desired consistency is achieved.

*Serving Size: One serving*

**Nutrition Facts (approximate per serving):**

- ❖ Calories: 150.
- ❖ Carbohydrate: 25 grams
- ❖ Fat: 3g
- ❖ Cholesterol: 0 mg.
- ❖ Sodium: 30 mg.
- ❖ Potassium: 400 mg.
- ❖ Phosphorus: 80 mg.
- ❖ Protein: 5 grams.
- ❖ Fiber: 3 grams.

### Cooking Tips:

- ❖ To make a thicker smoothie, use frozen fruit or add more ice cubes.
- ❖ Experiment with several varieties of milk or yogurt.
- ❖ Add a handful of spinach for an added dose of nutrition.
- ❖ Drizzle with honey or maple syrup to enhance sweetness.

### Health Benefits:

- ❖ Strawberries and bananas are high in antioxidants and vitamins.
- ❖ Greek yogurt contains protein and calcium.
- ❖ This smoothie is both refreshing and hydrating.
- ❖ It contains a high fiber content, which is beneficial to digestive health.

## 4. Berry Blast Smoothie

This Berry Blast Smoothie is both refreshing and nutritious, full of antioxidants and vitamins.

The bright combination of berries results in a delightful and energizing treat. This smoothie is a delicious way to start the day, whether as a quick breakfast or a healthy snack.

- ❖ *Preparation time: 5 minutes*
- ❖ *Cooking Time: N/A*
- ❖ *Total time: 5 minutes.*

### Ingredients:

- ❖ 1 cup mixed berries (strawberries, raspberries, blueberries)
- ❖ 1/2 cup Greek yogurt.
- ❖ 1/2 cup of unsweetened almond milk.
- ❖ One tablespoon honey (optional)
- ❖ Ice cubes

### Instructions:

- ❖ In a blender, combine mixed berries, Greek yogurt, almond milk, and honey (if desired).
- ❖ Blend until smooth and creamy.
- ❖ Blend in ice cubes until desired consistency.

### *Serving Size: One serving*

### Nutrition Facts (approximate per serving):

- ❖ Calories: 150.
- ❖ Carbohydrate: 25 grams
- ❖ Fat: 3g
- ❖ Cholesterol: 0 mg.
- ❖ Sodium: 30 mg.
- ❖ Potassium: 400 mg.
- ❖ Phosphorus: 80 mg.
- ❖ Protein: 5 grams.
- ❖ Fiber: 3 grams.

### Cooking Tips:

- ❖ To make a thicker smoothie, use frozen fruit or add extra ice cubes.
- ❖ Experiment with several kinds of yogurt and milk.
- ❖ Add a handful of spinach for extra nutrients.
- ❖ Drizzle with honey or maple syrup to enhance sweetness.
- ❖ Garnish with fresh berries or a mint leaf for display.

### Health Benefits:

- ❖ Berries are loaded with antioxidants and micronutrients.
- ❖ Greek yogurt contains protein and calcium.
- ❖ This smoothie is both refreshing and hydrating.
- ❖ It contains a high fiber content, which is beneficial to digestive health.

## 5. Low Potassium Green Smoothie

A low-potassium green smoothie is a delightful and nutritious option for those watching their potassium intake. This smoothie is packed with critical vitamins, minerals, and antioxidants, making it a tasty approach to boost overall health.

- ❖ *Preparation time: 10 minutes*
- ❖ *Cooking Time: N/A*
- ❖ *Total time: 10 minutes.*

## Ingredients:

- ❖ 1 cup spinach.
- ❖ 1/2 cucumber, peeled and sliced.
- ❖ 1/2 green bell pepper, chopped.
- ❖ 1/4 cup low-potassium fruit (such as berries or pineapple)
- ❖ 1/2 cup of unsweetened almond milk.
- ❖ 1 tablespoon of lemon juice.
- ❖ 1/4 teaspoon of ginger (optional)
- ❖ Ice cubes

## Instructions:

- ❖ Mix spinach, cucumber, green bell pepper, low-potassium fruit, almond milk, lemon juice, and ginger in a blender.

- ❖ Blend until smooth and creamy.
- ❖ Add ice cubes and blend again until the desired consistency is achieved.

*Serving Size: One serving*

**Nutrition Facts (approximate per serving):**

- ❖ Calories: 100.
- ❖ Carbohydrate: 15 grams
- ❖ Fat: 3g
- ❖ Cholesterol: 0 mg.
- ❖ Sodium: 30 mg.
- ❖ Potassium: 150 mg.
- ❖ Phosphorus: 50 mg.
- ❖ Protein: 3 grams.
- ❖ Fiber: 3 grams.

**Cooking Tips:**

- ❖ Experiment with various low-potassium fruits and veggies.
- ❖ Add a scoop of plant-based protein powder to make the smoothie more satisfying.
- ❖ Use a natural sweetener, such as stevia, to achieve a sweeter taste.
- ❖ If your smoothie is too thick, add more almond milk.

**Health Benefits:**

- ❖ Loaded with vitamins, minerals, and antioxidants.
- ❖ It is low in potassium, making it ideal for people who have dietary restrictions.
- ❖ Provides hydration and promotes overall health.
- ❖ A refreshing and nutritious way to enhance your veggie intake.

# Vegetables and Sides Recipes

## 1. Sautéed Spinach with Garlic

Sautéed spinach with garlic is a tasty and nutritious side dish. This quick and easy meal emphasizes the fresh taste of spinach while adding a hint of garlic for flavor. It's a flexible side dish that pairs well with a number of main courses.

- *Preparation time: 5 minutes*
- *Cook time: 5 minutes.*
- *Total time: 10 minutes.*

### Ingredients:

- 1 bunch of fresh spinach, washed and stemmed
- 2 garlic cloves, minced
- 1 tablespoon of olive oil.
- Add salt and pepper to taste.

### Instructions:

- In a large skillet, heat olive oil over medium heat.
- Sauté garlic for about 30 seconds, until aromatic.
- Add the spinach to the skillet in batches and stir constantly until wilted.
- Season with salt and pepper to taste.

*Serving size: one cup.*

**Nutrition Facts (approximate per serving):**

- Calories: 40.
- Carbohydrate: 5 grams
- Fat: 2g
- Cholesterol: 0 mg.
- Sodium: 100 mg.
- Potassium: 400 mg.
- Phosphorus: 50 mg.
- Protein: 3 grams.
- Fiber: 2 grams.

### Cooking Tips:

- A squeeze of lemon juice at the end will give the dish a deeper flavor.
- Serve immediately, while the spinach is still warm.
- For a spicy kick, add red pepper flakes.
- Fresh spinach provides the greatest flavor and texture.

### Health Benefits:

- Spinach is loaded with vitamins, minerals, and antioxidants.
- This meal contains little calories and fat, making it a nutritious side dish.
- Garlic has several health advantages, including anti-inflammatory effects.

## 2. Garlic Mashed Cauliflower

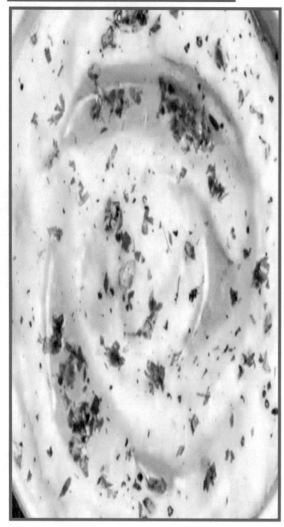

Garlic mashed cauliflower is a low-carb and gluten-free alternative to classic mashed potatoes. This creamy and tasty meal is nutrient-dense and may be served as a side or main entrée.

- ❖ *Preparation time: 15 minutes*
- ❖ *Cook time: 20 minutes.*
- ❖ *Total time: 35 minutes.*

**Ingredients:**

- ❖ 1 large head of cauliflower, chopped into florets
- ❖ 2 garlic cloves, minced
- ❖ 1/4 cup olive oil.
- ❖ 1/4 cup grated parmesan cheese.
- ❖ Add salt and pepper to taste.
- ❖ Optional: 1/4 cup of unsweetened almond milk

**Instructions:**

- ❖ Steam the cauliflower florets for 10-12 minutes, or until they are tender. Drain well.
- ❖ In a small skillet, cook the garlic in olive oil until aromatic.
- ❖ In a food processor, combine the cooked cauliflower, sautéd garlic, Parmesan cheese, salt, and pepper. Pulse until you reach your desired consistency.
- ❖ If needed, add a small amount of almond milk to achieve the appropriate creaminess.

*Serving size: one cup.*

**Nutrition Facts (approximate per serving):**

- ❖ Calories: 100.
- ❖ Carbohydrate: 5 grams
- ❖ Fat: 7g
- ❖ Cholesterol: 0 mg.
- ❖ Sodium: 100 mg.
- ❖ Potassium: 400 mg.
- ❖ Phosphorus: 50 mg.
- ❖ Protein: 3 grams.
- ❖ Fiber: 3 grams.

**Cooking Tips:**

- ❖ Replace almond milk with heavy cream for a fuller flavor.
- ❖ Garnish with fresh herbs, such as dill or chives.
- ❖ Serve as a side dish or as a low-carb foundation for other dishes.
- ❖ Refrigerate leftovers in an airtight jar for up to three days.

**Health Benefits:**

- ❖ Cauliflower is a low-carb veggie full of vitamins and minerals.
- ❖ This meal is a low-calorie alternative to mashed potatoes.
- ❖ Garlic contains many health advantages, including anti-inflammatory effects.
- ❖ A versatile side dish that can be consumed as part of a nutritious diet.

## 3. Quinoa Pilaf

Quinoa pilaf is a versatile and healthful dish that may be served as either a main course or a side dish. This meal pairs quinoa's airy texture with the savory aromas of aromatic veggies and herbs.

- ❖ *Preparation time: 10 minutes*
- ❖ *Cook time: 20 minutes.*
- ❖ *Total time: 30 minutes.*

**Ingredients:**

- ❖ 1 cup of quinoa, rinsed
- ❖ 1 onion, chopped
- ❖ 1 green bell pepper, chopped
- ❖ 2 garlic cloves, minced
- ❖ 2 cups veggie broth.
- ❖ 1/4 cup dried cranberries.
- ❖ 1/4 cup chopped fresh parsley.
- ❖ Add salt and pepper to taste.

**Instructions:**

- ❖ In a large skillet, sauté the onion and green pepper in olive oil until tender. Cook for a further 30 seconds after adding the garlic.
- ❖ Stir in the quinoa and heat for 1 minute, until lightly toasted.
- ❖ Pour in the vegetable broth, bring to a boil, then reduce the heat, cover, and simmer for 20 minutes, or until the liquid is absorbed and the quinoa is fluffy.
- ❖ Stir in the dried cranberries and fresh parsley. Season with salt and pepper to taste.

*Serving size: one cup.*

**Nutrition Facts (approximate per serving):**

- ❖ Calories: 200.
- ❖ Carbohydrate: 35 grams
- ❖ Fat: 3g
- ❖ Cholesterol: 0 mg.
- ❖ Sodium: 150 mg.
- ❖ Potassium: 300 mg.
- ❖ Phosphorus: 150 mg.
- ❖ Protein: 8 grams.
- ❖ Fiber: 5 grams.

**Cooking Tips:**

- ❖ To increase taste, toast the quinoa in a small bit of olive oil before adding the vegetables.
- ❖ Experiment with other herbs and spices, such cumin, coriander, and dill.
- ❖ Quinoa pilaf can be served as a side dish or as the main course alongside grilled chicken or fish.
- ❖ Refrigerate leftovers in an airtight jar for up to three days.

**Health Benefits:**

- ❖ Quinoa is a complete protein that contains all essential amino acids.
- ❖ This dish contains fiber and antioxidants.
- ❖ It is a low-fat, cholesterol-free choice.
- ❖ Quinoa pilaf is a versatile and healthful dish that can be served hot or cold.

## 4. Baked Sweet Potato Fries.

Baked sweet potato fries provide a healthier alternative to classic french fries while maintaining a delightful crunch. These fries are naturally sweet and high in nutrients, making them a tasty and guilt-free snack or side dish.

- ❖ *Preparation time: 15 minutes*
- ❖ *Cooking time: 25-30 minutes.*
- ❖ *Total Time: 40-45 minutes.*

## Ingredients:

- ❖ 1 huge sweet potato.
- ❖ 1 tablespoon of olive oil.
- ❖ 1/2 teaspoon of garlic powder.
- ❖ 1/4 teaspoon paprika.
- ❖ Add salt and pepper to taste.

## Instructions:

- ❖ Preheat the oven to 400° F (200° C). Line a baking sheet with parchment paper.
- ❖ Peel the sweet potato and cut it into long, evenly sized fries.
- ❖ In a large mixing basin, combine the sweet potato fries with the olive oil, garlic powder, paprika, salt, and pepper.
- ❖ Place the fries in a single layer on the prepared baking sheet.
- ❖ Bake for 25-30 minutes, or until golden brown and crispy. Flip the fries halfway through cooking.

*Serving size: 1/2 cup.*

**Nutrition Facts (approximate per serving):**

- ❖ Calories: 100.
- ❖ Carbohydrate: 20g
- ❖ Fat: 4g
- ❖ Cholesterol: 0 mg.
- ❖ Sodium: 50 mg.
- ❖ Potassium: 400 mg.
- ❖ Phosphorus: 50 mg.
- ❖ Protein: 2 grams.
- ❖ Fiber: 3 grams.

## Cooking Tips:

- ❖ To get extra crispy fries, soak the sweet potato fries in cold water for 30 minutes before baking.
- ❖ Experiment with other seasonings like chili powder, cumin, and cayenne pepper.

- ❖ Serve alongside your favorite dipping sauce, such as ketchup, ranch, or hummus.
- ❖ Keep leftovers in an airtight jar for up to two days.

## Health Benefits:

- ❖ Sweet potatoes are loaded with vitamins, minerals, and fiber.
- ❖ Baked sweet potato fries are a healthier option than typical fried fries.
- ❖ This recipe is low in both fat and cholesterol.
- ❖ A tasty and enjoyable snack or side dish.

## 5. Roasted Brussels sprouts.

Roasted Brussels sprouts are a tasty and healthful side dish that has become increasingly popular in recent years.

This easy preparation procedure turns an often-overlooked vegetable into a crispy and tasty snack.

- ❖ *Preparation time: 10 minutes*
- ❖ *Cooking time: 25-30 minutes.*
- ❖ *Total Time: 35-40 minutes.*

## Ingredients:

- ❖ 1 pound of Brussels sprouts, cut and halved
- ❖ 2 tablespoons of olive oil.
- ❖ 1/2 teaspoon of salt.
- ❖ 1/4 teaspoon of black pepper.

## Instructions:

- ❖ Preheat the oven to 400° F (200° C). Line a baking sheet with parchment paper.
- ❖ In a large mixing basin, toss Brussels sprouts with olive oil, salt, and pepper until thoroughly coated.
- ❖ Spread the Brussels sprouts in a single layer on the prepared baking sheet.
- ❖ Roast for 25-30 minutes, or until golden brown and delicious. Flip halfway through.

*Serving size: 1/2 cup.*

## Nutrition Facts (approximate per serving):

- ❖ Calories: 40.
- ❖ Carbs: 6g
- ❖ Fat: 2g
- ❖ Cholesterol: 0 mg.
- ❖ Sodium: 100 mg.
- ❖ Potassium: 300 mg.
- ❖ Phosphorus: 50 mg.
- ❖ Protein: 2 grams.
- ❖ Fiber: 2 grams.

## Cooking Tips:

- ❖ Before roasting, sprinkle with red pepper flakes or garlic powder for added flavor.
- ❖ To add a tangy edge, drizzle with balsamic glaze or lemon-tahini dressing.
- ❖ Drizzle with maple syrup or honey before roasting for added flavor depth.
- ❖ Refrigerate leftovers in an airtight jar for up to three days.

## Health Benefits:

- ❖ Brussels sprouts are loaded with vitamins, minerals, and fiber.
- ❖ This recipe is minimal in calories and fat, making it a nutritious side dish.
- ❖ Roasting increases the natural sweetness of Brussels sprouts.
- ❖ A versatile vegetable that may be added to a variety of dishes.

## 6. Steamed asparagus with lemon

Steamed asparagus with lemon is a simple yet attractive side dish that highlights the vegetables' inherent flavor. This simple and healthful meal emphasizes the asparagus's bright, fresh flavor, with lemon juice adding a zesty edge.

- *Preparation time: 5 minutes*
- *Cooking Time: 5–7 minutes*
- *Total time: 10 to 12 minutes*

### Ingredients:

- 1 pound of fresh, trimmed asparagus
- 1 lemon juiced
- Add salt and pepper to taste.

### Instructions:

- Heat a big saucepan of salted water to a boil.
- While the water is heated, cut the asparagus spears' woody ends.
- Once the water has boiled, add the asparagus and cook for 5-7 minutes, or until tender-crisp.
- Drain the asparagus and immediately place in a serving dish.
- Squeeze fresh lemon juice over the asparagus and season with salt and pepper. Serve hot.

*Serving size: one cup.*

**Nutrition Facts (approximate per serving):**

- Calories: 25.
- Carbs: 3g
- Fat: 0.5g
- Cholesterol: 0 mg.
- Sodium: 10 mg.
- Potassium: 300 mg.
- Phosphorus: 50 mg.
- Protein: 2 grams.
- Fiber: 2 grams.

**Cooking Tips:**

- Drizzle with olive oil before serving to add depth of flavor.
- For added spice, sprinkle with red pepper flakes.
- To keep the asparagus' beautiful green color, shock it in ice water after steaming.
- Serve as a side dish alongside grilled fish or poultry.

**Health Benefits:**

- Asparagus is a low-calorie, nutrient-dense vegetable.
- It is rich in vitamins A, C, and K.
- This easy preparation procedure maintains the asparagus' natural flavor and nutrients.
- A pleasant and nutritious side dish alternative.

# Main Dishes

## 1. Baked cod with lemon

Baked cod with lemon is a simple but tasty dish high in protein and omega-3 fatty acids. The delicate white fish complements the bright and tart lemon for a delicious and nutritious dinner.

- ❖ *Preparation time: 10 minutes*
- ❖ *Cook time: 15-20 minutes.*
- ❖ *Total Time: 25-30 minutes.*

### Ingredients:

- ❖ 4 cod filets (about 6 ounces each)
- ❖ 1 lemon, zested and squeezed
- ❖ 2 tablespoons of olive oil.
- ❖ 1 clove garlic, minced
- ❖ 1/2 teaspoon of dried dill.
- ❖ Add salt and pepper to taste.

### Instructions:

- ❖ Preheat the oven to 400° F (200° C). Line a baking sheet with parchment paper.
- ❖ In a small bowl, mix together lemon zest, lemon juice, olive oil, garlic, dill, salt, and pepper.
- ❖ Rub the lemon mixture onto the fish filets.
- ❖ Place the fish filets on the prepared baking sheet.
- ❖ Bake for 15-20 minutes, or until the fish is readily flaked with a fork.

*Serving Size: One fish filet.*

**Nutrition Facts (approximate per serving):**

- ❖ Calories: 200.
- ❖ Carbs: 2g
- ❖ Fat: 10g
- ❖ Cholesterol: 70 mg.
- ❖ Sodium: 100 mg.
- ❖ Potassium: 300 mg.
- ❖ Phosphorus: 150 mg.
- ❖ Protein: 25 grams.
- ❖ Fiber: 1 g.

### Cooking Tips:

- ❖ To round up the dinner, serve with roasted veggies or a green salad.
- ❖ Before serving, sprinkle with fresh parsley for added taste.
- ❖ To keep the fish from drying out, avoid overcooking.
- ❖ Instead of olive oil, use butter to have a deeper flavor.

### Health Benefits:

- ❖ Cod is an excellent source of protein and omega-3 fatty acids.
- ❖ Lemon gives vitamin C while also adding a vivid flavor.
- ❖ This recipe is minimal in calories and fat, making it a healthier option.
- ❖ A quick and nutritious meal alternative.

## 2. Vegetarian Stuffed Peppers

Vegetarian stuffed peppers make a filling and tasty main meal. This dish is both filling and nutritious, thanks to its vegetables, grains, and protein content. The mix of sweet bell peppers and savory stuffing results in a tasty and colorful dish.

- ❖ *Preparation time: 30 minutes*
- ❖ *Cook time: 45 minutes.*
- ❖ *Total time: 75 minutes.*

**Ingredients:**

- ❖ 4 huge bell peppers.
- ❖ 1 cup brown rice, cooked
- ❖ 1 can (15 ounces) of black beans, washed and drained
- ❖ 1 onion, chopped
- ❖ 1 green bell pepper, chopped
- ❖ 2 garlic cloves, minced
- ❖ 1 teaspoon of chili powder.
- ❖ 1/2 teaspoon cumin.
- ❖ 1/4 cup corn kernels.
- ❖ 1/4 cup chopped fresh cilantro.
- ❖ 1/2 cup shredded cheddar cheese (optional).

**Instructions:**

- ❖ Preheat the oven to 375° Fahrenheit (190° Celsius).
- ❖ Cut bell peppers in half lengthwise, and remove the seeds and membranes. Place upside down on a baking pan and cook for 10-15 minutes, or until somewhat softened.
- ❖ While the peppers are roasting, sauté the onion and green bell pepper in a large skillet until tender. Add the garlic and heat for another 30 seconds.
- ❖ Stir in the cooked rice, black beans, chili powder, cumin, corn, and cilantro. Cook for 5 minutes to blend the flavors.
- ❖ Fill the roasted pepper halves with rice mixture. If desired, add shredded cheese on top.
- ❖ Bake for 20-25 minutes, or until the peppers are soft and the cheese has melted (if used).

*Serving Size: One stuffed pepper.*

**Nutrition Facts (approximate per serving):**

- ❖ Calories: 300.
- ❖ Carbohydrate: 40 grams
- ❖ Fat: 5g
- ❖ Cholesterol: 0 mg.
- ❖ Sodium: 300 mg.
- ❖ Potassium: 600 mg.
- ❖ Phosphorus: 150 mg.
- ❖ Protein: 12 grams.
- ❖ Fiber: 8 grams.

**Cooking Tips:**

- ❖ For a hotter filling, use jalapeño peppers or red pepper flakes.
- ❖ Use a variety of beans, including kidney and pinto beans.
- ❖ Serve alongside a side salad or a dollop of Greek yogurt.
- ❖ For a vegan variant, leave out the cheese or use a vegan cheese substitute.

**Health Benefits:**

- ❖ This dish has plant-based protein and fiber.
- ❖ Vegetables provide vitamins, minerals, and antioxidants.
- ❖ A delicious and nutritious supper that promotes overall wellness.
- ❖ Can be modified with your preferred vegetables and seasonings.

## 3. Spaghetti Squash Primavera

Spaghetti squash primavera is a nutritious and delectable low-carb alternative to regular spaghetti. This vivid dish is loaded with fresh veggies, making it a healthful and filling supper.

- ❖ *Preparation time: 15 minutes*
- ❖ *Cook time: 45 minutes.*
- ❖ *Total time: 60 minutes.*

**Ingredients:**

- ❖ 1 medium spaghetti squash.
- ❖ 1 tablespoon of olive oil.
- ❖ 1 onion, chopped
- ❖ 2 garlic cloves, minced
- ❖ 1 zucchini, sliced
- ❖ 1 yellow squash, sliced
- ❖ 1 red bell pepper, sliced
- ❖ 1 cup cherry tomatoes, halved
- ❖ 1/4 cup of fresh basil, chopped
- ❖ Add salt and pepper to taste.
- ❖ Parmesan cheese for serving is optional.

**Instructions:**

- ❖ Preheat the oven to 375° Fahrenheit (190° Celsius).
- ❖ Cut spaghetti squash in half lengthwise and remove the seeds. Place the sliced side down in a baking dish containing a little water. Bake for 45 minutes or until tender.
- ❖ While the squash is baking, warm the olive oil in a large skillet over medium heat. Sauté the onion and garlic until tender.
- ❖ Combine zucchini, yellow squash, and red bell pepper. Cook till tender crisp.
- ❖ After cooking the spaghetti squash, allow it to cool somewhat. Use a fork to separate the flesh into strands.
- ❖ Combine spaghetti squash and veggie combination. Stir in the fresh basil, salt, and pepper.
- ❖ Serve immediately, with optional Parmesan cheese.

*Serving Size: One serving*

**Nutrition Facts (approximate per serving):**

- ❖ Calories: 200.
- ❖ Carbohydrate: 25 grams
- ❖ Fat: 7g
- ❖ Cholesterol: 0 mg.
- ❖ Sodium: 150 mg.
- ❖ Potassium: 500 mg.
- ❖ Phosphorus: 100 mg.
- ❖ Protein: 5 grams.
- ❖ Fiber: 6 grams.

**Cooking Tips:**

- ❖ Add more veggies, such as mushrooms or spinach, for variety.
- ❖ For a creamier sauce, add a tiny bit of ricotta cheese or Greek yogurt.
- ❖ Serve over a bed of spinach or arugula for added nutrition.
- ❖ Experiment with different herbs and spices to create your own flavor.

**Health Benefits:**

- ❖ Spaghetti squash is a low-carb alternative to pasta that contains fiber and minerals.
- ❖ The vegetables in this recipe provide plenty of vitamins, minerals, and antioxidants.
- ❖ A light and pleasant supper with low calories and fat.
- ❖ A versatile base for adding different proteins, such as grilled chicken or shrimp.

## 4. Chicken and Vegetable Skewers

Chicken and veggie skewers are a tasty and nutritious grilling option. These skewers, loaded with protein and colorful vegetables, are ideal for a summer BBQ or a midweek dinner. The combination of flavors and textures results in a pleasant and delightful supper.

- ❖ *Preparation time: 30 minutes*
- ❖ *Cook time: 15-20 minutes.*
- ❖ *Total Time: 45-50 minutes.*

**Ingredients:**

- ❖ 1 pound of boneless, skinless chicken breasts cut into 1-inch cubes.
- ❖ 1 red bell pepper, sliced into 1 inch chunks.
- ❖ 1 yellow bell pepper (cut into 1-inch chunks)
- ❖ 1 onion, chopped into 1 inch pieces.
- ❖ 1 zucchini, sliced into 1 inch pieces.
- ❖ 1/4 cup olive oil.
- ❖ 2 teaspoons of lemon juice.
- ❖ 1 teaspoon of garlic powder.
- ❖ 1/2 teaspoon of onion powder.
- ❖ Add salt and pepper to taste.

**Instructions:**

- ❖ In a large bowl, add the chicken, bell peppers, onion, and zucchini.
- ❖ Mix together the olive oil, lemon juice, garlic powder, onion powder, salt, and pepper. Toss the chicken and vegetables with the sauce.
- ❖ Marinate for at least 30 minutes, but up to overnight.
- ❖ Preheat the grill to medium-high heat.
- ❖ Thread chicken and vegetables alternately onto skewers.
- ❖ Grill the skewers for 10-12 minutes, or until the chicken is thoroughly cooked and the vegetables are soft, flipping regularly.

*Serving Size: four skewers.*

**Nutrition Facts (approximate per serving):**

- ❖ Calories: 300.
- ❖ Carbohydrate: 20g
- ❖ Fat: 15g
- ❖ Cholesterol: 70 mg.
- ❖ Sodium: 250 mg.
- ❖ Potassium: 500 mg.
- ❖ Phosphorus: 150 mg.
- ❖ Protein: 25 grams.
- ❖ Fiber: 3 grams.

## Cooking Tips:

- ❖ Marinate the chicken and vegetables for an extended period of time to enhance their taste.
- ❖ Use metal skewers to cook evenly.
- ❖ Serve with rice or quinoa to complete the meal.
- ❖ Experiment with various vegetables such as mushrooms, cherry tomatoes, and pineapple.

## Health Benefits:

- ❖ This dish is rich in protein, vitamins, and minerals.
- ❖ Grilling is a healthy cooking method that retains nutrients.
- ❖ Chicken with vegetables make for a well-balanced lunch.
- ❖ A wonderful and gratifying way to eat grilled foods.

## 5. Grilled lamb chops

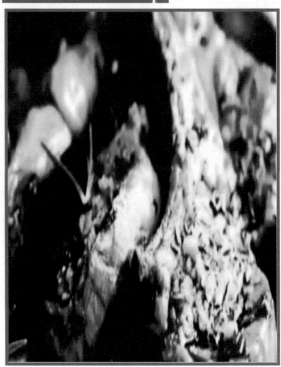

Grilled lamb chops are a tasty and satisfying dinner dish. This dish brings out the rich flavor of the lamb while allowing the natural juices to emerge. With a simple marinade and careful cooking, these chops are a delicious and attractive choice for any event.

- ❖ *Preparation time: 30 minutes*
- ❖ *Cook time: 10-15 minutes.*
- ❖ *Total time: 40-45 minutes.*

## Ingredients:

- ❖ 4 lamb chops (about 1 inch thick)
- ❖ 2 garlic cloves, minced
- ❖ 1 tablespoon of fresh rosemary, chopped
- ❖ 1 tablespoon of olive oil.
- ❖ 1 teaspoon of lemon zest.
- ❖ 1/2 teaspoon of salt.
- ❖ 1/4 teaspoon of black pepper.

## Instructions:

- ❖ In a small bowl, mix together the garlic, rosemary, olive oil, lemon zest, salt, and pepper.
- ❖ Rub the marinade over the lamb chops to ensure even covering.
- ❖ Allow the lamb chops to marinade for at least 30 minutes, or up to 2 hours in the refrigerator.
- ❖ Preheat the grill for medium-high heat.
- ❖ Grill lamb chops for 5-7 minutes per side, or to desired doneness (145°F for medium).
- ❖ Allow the lamb chops to rest for 5 minutes before serving.

*Serving size: one lamb chop.*

## Nutrition Facts (approximate per serving):

- ❖ Calories: 250.
- ❖ Carbohydrate: 0g
- ❖ Fat: 18g
- ❖ Cholesterol: 90 mg.
- ❖ Sodium: 150 mg.
- ❖ Potassium: 300 mg.
- ❖ Phosphorus: 150 mg.
- ❖ Protein: 25 grams.
- ❖ Fiber: 0 grams.

## Cooking Tips:

- ❖ Marinate the lamb chops overnight to enhance their taste.
- ❖ Use a meat thermometer to check that the lamb chops are cooked to the proper doneness.
- ❖ Serve alongside roasted veggies or a simple salad.
- ❖ To retain the fluids, allow the lamb chops to rest before chopping into them.

## Health Benefits:

- ❖ Lamb is an excellent source of protein and iron.
- ❖ This recipe is low in carbohydrates yet high in protein.
- ❖ Grilling is a healthy cooking method that lowers fat content.
- ❖ Enjoy as part of a well-balanced diet for maximum health.

## 6. Herb-crusted Pork Loin

Herb-crusted pork loin is a tasty and tender main course suitable for both a weeknight dinner and a special event. The combination of fresh herbs and spices results in a delectable crust that complements the succulent pork.

- ❖ *Preparation time: 15 minutes*
- ❖ *Cooking time: 45–50 minutes*
- ❖ *Total Time: 65-70 minutes.*

## Ingredients:

- ❖ 1 boneless pork loin roast (about 2-3 lbs)
- ❖ 1/4 cup olive oil.
- ❖ 2 tablespoons Dijon mustard.
- ❖ 2 garlic cloves, minced

- ❖ 2 teaspoons of fresh rosemary, chopped
- ❖ 2 tablespoons fresh thyme, chopped.
- ❖ 1 teaspoon of dried oregano.
- ❖ 1/2 teaspoon of salt.
- ❖ 1/4 teaspoon of black pepper.

## Instructions:

- ❖ Preheat the oven to 375° Fahrenheit (190° Celsius).
- ❖ In a small bowl, mix together olive oil, Dijon mustard, garlic, rosemary, thyme, oregano, salt, and pepper.
- ❖ Rub the herb mixture evenly over the pork loin to ensure even covering.
- ❖ Place the pork loin on a roasting rack inside a roasting pan.
- ❖ Roast for 45-50 minutes, or until a meat thermometer inserted in the thickest portion of the pork loin registers 145°F (63°C).
- ❖ Remove from the oven and allow it to rest for 10 minutes before slicing.

*Serving Size: 3 oz.*

**Nutrition Facts (approximate per serving):**

- ❖ Calories: 180
- ❖ Carbohydrate: 0g
- ❖ Fat: 12g
- ❖ Cholesterol: 80 mg.
- ❖ Sodium: 150 mg.
- ❖ Potassium: 300 mg.
- ❖ Phosphorus: 150 mg.
- ❖ Protein: 25 grams.
- ❖ Fiber: 0 grams.

**Cooking Tips:**

- ❖ Before roasting the pork loin, brown it in a skillet to get a crisp exterior.
- ❖ Add other herbs, such as sage or parsley, to the herb combination.
- ❖ To round out the dish, serve with roasted veggies or a side salad.
- ❖ Allow the pork to rest before carving to retain the juices.

**Health Benefits:**

- ❖ Pork loin is a lean protein source.
- ❖ This recipe is low in carbohydrates yet high in protein.
- ❖ The herb crust enhances flavor and provides antioxidants.
- ❖ A pleasant and savory main course choice.

# Chapter 5

## Tips and Resources

Managing CKD Stage 3 with nutrition is critical for preserving health and preventing additional kidney damage. This chapter offers practical advice and resources to help you make informed dietary decisions and enjoy a range of delicious, kidney-friendly meals. From grocery shopping to meal planning, cooking techniques, and portion control, these tips are intended to help seniors on their path to better kidney health.

## Grocery Shopping Guide for CKD

Grocery shopping with CKD Stage 3 necessitates careful preparation and informed decisions to ensure that you choose goods that meet your dietary requirements. Here are some important ideas to help you shop efficiently:

*1. Create a list:* Before going to the supermarket, make a detailed shopping list based on your weekly meal plan. This list can help you stay focused and avoid impulse purchases of harmful items.

*2. Read labels:* Become an expert in reading food labels. Look for data on sodium, potassium, and phosphorus levels. Select items labeled "low sodium," "no added salt," "low potassium," or "kidney-friendly."

*3. Choose fresh, whole foods wherever feasible:* Fresh fruits, vegetables, lean meats, and whole grains are generally lower in salt, potassium, and phosphorus than processed and packaged foods.

*4. Avoid processed foods:* Many processed foods include high quantities of salt and phosphorus additions. Avoid canned soups, freezer dinners, snacks, and deli meats. Instead, cook meals from scratch with fresh ingredients.

*5. Choose Low Potassium Fruits and Vegetables:* Choose fruits and vegetables that are low in potassium. Apples, berries, grapes, green beans, carrots, and cauliflower are all great selections. Limit potassium-rich foods such as bananas, oranges, potatoes, and tomatoes.

*6. Select lean proteins:* Lean protein sources include chicken, turkey, and fish, as well as plant-based proteins such as beans and lentils. Avoid processed meats because they are generally heavy in salt and phosphorus.

*7. Look for Phosphorus Additives:* Check ingredient lists for phosphorus additions, which are frequently included in processed foods and beverages. Avoid products that contain the term "phosphate."

*8. Limit dairy products:* Dairy products can have high levels of phosphorus. Choose low-phosphorus alternatives like almond milk or rice milk, and restrict your intake of cheese, yogurt, and milk.

*9. Hydrate wisely:* Choose beverages low in sodium and phosphorus. Water is the greatest choice, but you can also drink herbal teas and infused waters. Avoid sodas, sports drinks, and certain fruit juices that may contain excessive levels of potassium and phosphorus.

***10. Budget-Friendly Shopping:*** Eating kidney-friendly does not have to be pricey. Buy seasonal produce, seek for deals, and think about buying frozen fruits and vegetables, which are sometimes just as nutritious as fresh.

## 14-Day Meal Plan for CKD Stage 3

This 14-day meal plan is intended to help seniors with CKD Stage 3 manage their disease while eating a variety of delicious and kidney-friendly meals. Every day includes breakfast, lunch, supper, and snacks. The meals are designed to give necessary nutrients while limiting salt, potassium, and phosphorus consumption.

### Day 1
***Breakfast:*** Apple Cinnamon Oatmeal
***Lunch:*** Grilled Chicken Quinoa Salad
***Dinner:*** Baked Salmon with Herb Sauce

### Day 2
***Breakfast:*** Berry Smoothie
***Lunch:*** Turkey and Avocado Wrap
***Dinner:*** Grilled Tilapia with Brown Rice and Roasted Zucchini

### Day 3
***Breakfast:*** Scrambled Egg Whites with Spinach and Whole Wheat Toast
***Lunch:*** Lentil and Carrot Soup with a Small Side Salad

***Dinner:*** Herb-Roasted Chicken Breast with Mashed Cauliflower and Steamed Broccoli

### Day 4
***Breakfast:*** Greek Yogurt with Sliced Strawberries and Honey
***Lunch:*** Tuna Salad with Mixed Greens and a Lemon Vinaigrette
***Dinner:*** Baked Cod with Steamed Asparagus and Quinoa

### Day 5
***Breakfast:*** Whole Wheat Pancakes with Blueberries and a Drizzle of Maple Syrup
***Lunch:*** Chicken and Vegetable Stir-Fry with Brown Rice
***Dinner:*** Grilled Pork Tenderloin with Roasted Brussels Sprouts and Mashed Sweet Potatoes

### Day 6
***Breakfast:*** Smoothie Bowl
***Lunch:*** Quinoa and Black Bean Stuffed Peppers
***Dinner:*** Lemon Garlic Shrimp with Steamed Green Beans and Brown Rice

### Day 7
***Breakfast:*** Berry Oatmeal
***Lunch:*** Turkey Sandwich on Whole Wheat Bread with Lettuce, Tomato, and Avocado
***Dinner:*** Grilled Chicken with Steamed Broccoli and a Side of Quinoa

### Day 8
***Breakfast:*** Whole Wheat Toast with Avocado and a Poached Egg
***Lunch:*** Grilled Vegetable Salad

*Dinner:* Baked Lemon Herb Chicken Thighs with Roasted Cauliflower and Brown Rice

## Day 9

*Breakfast:* Smoothie
*Lunch:* Lentil Soup with a Small Side Salad
*Dinner:* Grilled Salmon with Quinoa and Steamed Asparagus

## Day 10

*Breakfast:* Scrambled Egg Whites with Sautéed Mushrooms and Spinach
*Lunch:* Turkey and Avocado Wrap
*Dinner:* Herb-Crusted Pork Loin with Roasted Brussels Sprouts and Mashed Sweet Potatoes

## Day 11

*Breakfast:* Greek Yogurt with Fresh Berries and Honey
*Lunch:* Chicken Caesar Salad
*Dinner:* Grilled Shrimp with Brown Rice and Steamed Broccoli

## Day 12

*Breakfast:* Oatmeal with Sliced Bananas and Almond Butter
*Lunch:* Tuna Salad with Mixed Greens and a Lemon Vinaigrette
*Dinner:* Baked Tilapia with Quinoa and Roasted Zucchini

## Day 13

*Breakfast:* Whole Wheat Pancakes with Sliced Strawberries
*Lunch:* Chicken and Vegetable Stir-Fry with Brown Rice

*Dinner:* Grilled Pork Tenderloin with Roasted Brussels Sprouts and Mashed Cauliflower

## Day 14

*Breakfast:* Smoothie Bowl
*Lunch:* Quinoa and Black Bean Stuffed Peppers
*Dinner:* Lemon Garlic Shrimp with Steamed Green Beans and Brown Rice

## Meal Planning Tips:

Effective meal planning is essential for controlling CKD Stage 3. It helps you receive the essential nutrients while adhering to your dietary restrictions. Here are some meal planning suggestions to keep you on track:

**1. Plan ahead:** Set aside time every week to organize your meals. Choose what you will eat at breakfast, lunch, dinner, and snacks. Having a strategy lowers the likelihood of making poor eating choices.

**2. Batch cooking:** Prepare larger quantities of kidney-friendly foods and keep them in the fridge or freezer. Batch cooking saves time and ensures that you always have nutritious meals ready to go.

**3. Variety is key:** Include a variety of meals in your meal plan to ensure you obtain a wide range of nutrients. To keep your meals exciting and balanced, rotate between fruits, vegetables, meats, and grains.

**4. Portion Control:** Plan your meals with suitable serving sizes. Use smaller dishes and bowls to help limit portion sizes and avoid overeating. Refer to the portion size suggestions included later in this chapter.

**5. Use leftovers:** Include leftovers in your food plan. Leftover veggies can be used into soups or salads, while cooked meats can be utilized in sandwiches or stir-fries. This lowers food waste and saves money.

**6. Preparing Ingredients in Advance:** Preparing items ahead of time will make dinner preparation quicker and easier. Wash and chop vegetables, marinade meats, and prepare spices and herbs. Store prepared materials in airtight containers.

**7. Stay hydrated:** Include beverages in your meal plan to keep you hydrated. Remember to restrict liquids high in potassium and phosphorus. Water, herbal teas, and flavored waters are excellent choices.

**8. Adjust as needed:** Maintain flexibility and change your eating plan as needed. If you discover that particular foods do not agree with you or if your dietary requirements change, make the necessary changes to your plan.

## Cooking Tips for Seniors

When done correctly, cooking kidney-friendly foods may be both pleasurable and gratifying. Here are some ways to help elders cook nutritious, delicious meals:

**1. Simple and safe:** Choose basic recipes with a few steps to make cooking less intimidating. Make your kitchen safe by keeping it organized and utilizing products made for seniors, such as ergonomic knives and easy-to-grip utensils.

**2. Flavor without salt:** Enhance the flavor of your meals without adding salt. To enhance flavor, use herbs, spices, garlic, lemon juice, and vinegar. Fresh herbs, such as basil, cilantro, and parsley, can add lively tastes to your dishes.

**3. Healthy Cooking Methods:** Choose healthy cooking methods including baking, grilling, steaming, and stir-frying. These approaches conserve nutrition while reducing the need for additional fats and sodium.

**4. Batch-cooking and freezing:** Prepare larger batches of kidney-friendly recipes and freeze in individual servings. This not only saves time, but also guarantees that you have nutritious meals available when you need them.

**5. Cooking for one or two:** If you're cooking for yourself or a small family, look into recipes that can be easily scaled down. Cook in larger batches and freeze the leftovers for future meals.

**6. Use fresh ingredients:** Whenever feasible, utilize fresh ingredients to increase flavor and nutritional value. Fresh fruits, vegetables, and herbs can enhance and improve the flavor of your cuisine.

**7. Experiment with recipes:** Do not be hesitant to try new recipes and ingredients. This cookbook includes a selection of kidney-friendly recipes to inspire you. Trying different meals makes your diet exciting and tasty.

**8. Stay Organized:** Keep your kitchen organized to increase cooking efficiency. Keep frequently used things within reach and mark containers so you can find what you need fast.

## Managing Portion Sizes

Proper portion management is essential for treating CKD Stage 3. It helps to control nutrient intake and prevent overeating. Here are some suggestions for regulating portion sizes effectively:

**1. Use small plates and bowls:** Using smaller dishes and bowls can help with portion control by making servings appear larger. This can help you avoid overeating and keep to the recommended portion amounts.

**2. Measure portions:** Use measuring cups, spoons, and a food scale to correctly measure quantities. This ensures that you consume the appropriate amounts of each food type.

**3. Follow the Serving Size Guidelines:** Refer to the recipe's serving size instructions and nutritional facts. Follow these guidelines to maintain a balanced diet and avoid consuming too much salt, potassium, and phosphorus.

**4. Mindful eating:** Pay attention to hunger and fullness indicators to cultivate mindful eating skills. Eating deliberately and savoring each bite can help you feel full with lesser servings.

**5. Divide and store:** Divide larger meals into individual servings before eating. Store leftovers in portioned containers so that future meals are convenient and correctly sized.

**6. Balance Your Plate:** Fill half of your plate with veggies, one-fourth with lean protein, and the remaining quarter with whole grains or starchy vegetables. This balanced approach guarantees that you receive a range of nutrients in adequate proportions.

**7. Snack Smart:** Small, kidney-friendly snacks are ideal for satisfying appetite between meals. To avoid mindlessly consuming big amounts of snacks, split them out beforehand. Fruit slices, veggie sticks with hummus, or a handful of almonds (if your nutritionist permits) are all healthy options.

**8. Dine Out:** When eating out, be mindful of portion sizes. Many restaurant servings exceed the required size. Consider splitting a dish with a friend or ordering a to-go container to keep half for later.

## Conversion Charts For Measuring Ingredients

**Here are some popular conversions to aid you in the kitchen:**

*Volume conversions:*

- ❖ 1 teaspoon (tsp) equals five milliliters (ml).
- ❖ 1 tablespoon (tbsp) equals 3 teaspoons = 15 milliliters.

- ❖ 1 fluid ounce (fl oz) equals 2 tablespoons = 30 milliliters.
- ❖ 1 cup (c) equals eight fluid ounces (240 milliliters).
- ❖ 1 pint (pt) equals two cups (16 fluid ounces) or 480 milliliters.
- ❖ 1 quart (qt) equals four cups, two pints, 32 fluid ounces, or 960 milliliters.
- ❖ 1 gallon (gal) equals 4 quarts, 16 cups, 128 fluid ounces, or 3,840 milliliters.

### *Weight conversions:*

- ❖ 1 ounce (oz) equals 28 grams (g).
- ❖ 1 pound (lb) is 16 ounces or 454 grams.
- ❖ 1 kilogram (kg) equals 1,000 grams, or 2.2 pounds.

### *Temperature conversions:*

- ❖ To convert Fahrenheit to Celsius, use the formula $(°F - 32) × 5/9 = °C$.
- ❖ To convert Celsius to Fahrenheit, use $(°C × 9/5) + 32$.

### *Common Ingredient Conversions:*

- ❖ 1 cup flour equals 120 grams.
- ❖ 1 cup sugar equals 200 grams.
- ❖ 1 cup brown sugar equals 220 grams.
- ❖ 1 cup powdered sugar equals 120 grams.
- ❖ 1 cup butter equals 227 grams (about two sticks).
- ❖ 1 cup water equals 240 grams.
- ❖ 1 cup milk equals 240 grams.
- ❖ 1 cup yogurt is 245 grams.
- ❖ 1 cup (uncooked) rice equals 200 grams
- ❖ 1 cup of oats equals 90 grams.

- ❖ 1 cup honey is 340 grams.
- ❖ 1 cup oil equals 220 grams.

## Practical Tips for Using Conversion Tables

**1. Keep a copy handy:** Print a copy of these conversion tables and keep it in your kitchen for easy reference. This saves time and ensures that recipes are prepared accurately.

**2. Use Digital Tools:** Consider utilizing digital instruments such as kitchen scales and measuring spoons to get precise measurements. Many kitchen scales can convert between grams and ounces, making it easier to follow recipes from various sources.

**3. Adapt recipes:** When converting recipes, pay attention to ingredient ratios to ensure the dish's integrity. If a recipe specifies a weight or volume, use these conversion tables to adjust it to your preferred measurements.

**4. Double-check conversions:** When in doubt, double-check your conversions to prevent errors. Accurate measures are critical to the success of kidney-friendly meals, especially when dealing with nutrients like salt, potassium, and phosphorus.

**5. Adjust for elevation:** If you reside at a higher height, you may need to change your measures and cooking times. High elevations can have an impact on recipe results, so consult altitude-specific cooking tips as needed.

# Conclusion

Starting the journey of treating CKD Stage 3 might be difficult, but it is also an opportunity to regain control of your health and enhance your quality of life.

This cookbook is intended to be your reliable companion on your journey. We hope that by providing you with the necessary tools, knowledge, and recipes for following a kidney-friendly diet, you will find this journey both fun and manageable.

## *Empowerment via Knowledge:*

Understanding the complexities of CKD and the critical role nutrition plays in controlling the condition is the first step toward empowerment.

Armed with this knowledge, you may make informed decisions that will benefit your health. This cookbook is more than simply a collection of recipes; it is a thorough guide that will help you learn how to take control of your health.

## *Delicious and Nutritious Recipes:*

We think that eating properly should never entail giving up flavor or fun. The recipes in this cookbook have been carefully created to fulfill the nutritional requirements of CKD Stage 3 while also being delicious and enjoyable.

These meals, which range from robust breakfasts to delightful feasts and everything in between, are intended to bring joy to your table while also providing fuel to your body.

## *Practical Tips for Daily Life:*

Beyond the recipes, this cookbook contains useful suggestions and tools to help you in your daily life. Whether it's grocery shopping, meal planning, cooking techniques, or portion control, these tips are designed to make your life easier and your diet more successful.

By incorporating these suggestions into your daily routine, you can establish a sustainable lifestyle that promotes kidney health and overall wellness.

## *A supportive Community:*

Remember that you are not alone on this path. Seek assistance from family, friends, and healthcare professionals. Join communities and support groups to share your experiences and learn from others going through similar issues.

Together, we can build a supportive community that promotes health and happiness.

## *A commitment to Your Health:*

Your health is your most important possession. By following the instructions in this cookbook, you are committing to yourself and your well-being.

Every meal you prepare, every conscious decision you make, is a step toward improved health. Celebrate your progress, no matter how modest, and be inspired by the positive improvements you observe in your life.

### Looking Forward

As you continue down this route, start trying different dishes and techniques. Stay curious, knowledgeable, and committed to your health.

This cookbook is only the beginning of your road to controlling CKD Stage 3 and living a full, vibrant life.

***Thank You For Allowing Us To Share Your Journey.***

***We Hope This Cookbook Becomes A Valuable Resource In Your Kitchen, Motivating You To Prepare Kidney-Friendly Recipes That Are Also Delicious.***

***Here's To Your Health And Happiness, One Meal At A Time.***

# Bonus Section

## Bonus 1: Email Of Consultation

**Dear Valued Reader,**

Thank you for purchasing and reading the **"CKD Stage 3 Cookbook for Seniors."** We hope this book has provided you with valuable information, delicious recipes, and practical advice to help you manage your kidney health effectively.

Your feedback is extremely important to us, and we would be grateful if you could take the time to post a **FAVORABLE REVIEW.** Let us know what you found most helpful in the book—whether it was the variety of recipes, the meal planning tips, or the helpful hints and resources.

As a token of our appreciation, we are offering you an additional consultation via email. If you have any questions or concerns regarding the book, the CKD diet, or kidney health in general, please feel free to reach out to us at hmillerelva@gmail.com. I am more than happy to assist and support you on your health journey.

*Thank you for your continued support and for being a valued member of our community. Your positive rating and feedback allow us to continue providing valuable resources for others managing CKD.*

**Warm Regards,**

Elva H. Miller

## Bonus 2: Exercise for Seniors with CKD, Glossary of CKD-Friendly Ingredients, and Tips for Staying Hydrated Safely

**To claim these bonuses with ease, kindly scan the QR code provided above.**

**Thank you for choosing our book, and we wish you the best on your journey to better health!**

# Meal Planner Journal

# Meal Planner Journal

**Monday**

| Breakfast | Lunch | Dinner |
|---|---|---|
| | | |

**Tuesday**

| Breakfast | Lunch | Dinner |
|---|---|---|
| | | |

**Wednesday**

| Breakfast | Lunch | Dinner |
|---|---|---|
| | | |

**Thursday**

| Breakfast | Lunch | Dinner |
|---|---|---|
| | | |

**Friday**

| Breakfast | Lunch | Dinner |
|---|---|---|
| | | |

**SaturdAY/sUNDAY**

Breakfast

Lunch

Dinner

**Note**

# Meal Planner Journal

**Monday**

Breakfast | Lunch | Dinner

**Tuesday**

Breakfast | Lunch | Dinner

**Wednesday**

Breakfast | Lunch | Dinner

**Thursday**

Breakfast | Lunch | Dinner

**Friday**

Breakfast | Lunch | Dinner

## SaturdAY/SUNDAY

Breakfast

Lunch

Dinner

## Note

# Meal Planner Journal

**Monday**

| Breakfast | Lunch | Dinner |
|---|---|---|

**Tuesday**

| Breakfast | Lunch | Dinner |
|---|---|---|

**Wednesday**

| Breakfast | Lunch | Dinner |
|---|---|---|

**Thursday**

| Breakfast | Lunch | Dinner |
|---|---|---|

**Friday**

| Breakfast | Lunch | Dinner |
|---|---|---|

## SaturdAY/SUNDAY

Breakfast

Lunch

Dinner

## Note

# Meal Planner Journal

**Monday**

| Breakfast | Lunch | Dinner |
|-----------|-------|--------|
|           |       |        |

**Tuesday**

| Breakfast | Lunch | Dinner |
|-----------|-------|--------|
|           |       |        |

**Wednesday**

| Breakfast | Lunch | Dinner |
|-----------|-------|--------|
|           |       |        |

**Thursday**

| Breakfast | Lunch | Dinner |
|-----------|-------|--------|
|           |       |        |

**Friday**

| Breakfast | Lunch | Dinner |
|-----------|-------|--------|
|           |       |        |

## SaturdAY/sUNDAY

Breakfast

Lunch

Dinner

## Note

# Meal Planner Journal

**Monday**

| Breakfast | Lunch | Dinner |
|---|---|---|
| | | |

**Tuesday**

| Breakfast | Lunch | Dinner |
|---|---|---|
| | | |

**Wednesday**

| Breakfast | Lunch | Dinner |
|---|---|---|
| | | |

**Thursday**

| Breakfast | Lunch | Dinner |
|---|---|---|
| | | |

**Friday**

| Breakfast | Lunch | Dinner |
|---|---|---|
| | | |

## SaturdAY/sUNDAY

Breakfast

Lunch

Dinner

## Note

# Meal Planner Journal

## Monday
| Breakfast | Lunch | Dinner |
|---|---|---|
| | | |

## Tuesday
| Breakfast | Lunch | Dinner |
|---|---|---|
| | | |

## Wednesday
| Breakfast | Lunch | Dinner |
|---|---|---|
| | | |

## Thursday
| Breakfast | Lunch | Dinner |
|---|---|---|
| | | |

## Friday
| Breakfast | Lunch | Dinner |
|---|---|---|
| | | |

## SaturdAY/sUNDAY

Breakfast

Lunch

Dinner

## Note

# Meal Planner Journal

## Monday

| Breakfast | Lunch | Dinner |
|---|---|---|
| | | |

## Tuesday

| Breakfast | Lunch | Dinner |
|---|---|---|
| | | |

## Wednesday

| Breakfast | Lunch | Dinner |
|---|---|---|
| | | |

## Thursday

| Breakfast | Lunch | Dinner |
|---|---|---|
| | | |

## Friday

| Breakfast | Lunch | Dinner |
|---|---|---|
| | | |

## SaturdAY/sUNDAY

Breakfast

Lunch

Dinner

## Note

# Meal Planner Journal

**Monday**

| Breakfast | Lunch | Dinner |
|---|---|---|
| | | |

**Tuesday**

| Breakfast | Lunch | Dinner |
|---|---|---|
| | | |

**Wednesday**

| Breakfast | Lunch | Dinner |
|---|---|---|
| | | |

**Thursday**

| Breakfast | Lunch | Dinner |
|---|---|---|
| | | |

**Friday**

| Breakfast | Lunch | Dinner |
|---|---|---|
| | | |

## SaturdAY/SUNDAY

Breakfast

Lunch

Dinner

## Note

# Meal Planner Journal

## Monday
| Breakfast | Lunch | Dinner |
|---|---|---|
| | | |

## Tuesday
| Breakfast | Lunch | Dinner |
|---|---|---|
| | | |

## Wednesday
| Breakfast | Lunch | Dinner |
|---|---|---|
| | | |

## Thursday
| Breakfast | Lunch | Dinner |
|---|---|---|
| | | |

## Friday
| Breakfast | Lunch | Dinner |
|---|---|---|
| | | |

## SaturdAY/sUNDAY

Breakfast

Lunch

Dinner

## Note

# Meal Planner Journal

**Monday**

| Breakfast | Lunch | Dinner |
|---|---|---|
| | | |

**Tuesday**

| Breakfast | Lunch | Dinner |
|---|---|---|
| | | |

**Wednesday**

| Breakfast | Lunch | Dinner |
|---|---|---|
| | | |

**Thursday**

| Breakfast | Lunch | Dinner |
|---|---|---|
| | | |

**Friday**

| Breakfast | Lunch | Dinner |
|---|---|---|
| | | |

**SaturdAY/sUNDAY**

Breakfast

Lunch

Dinner

**Note**

Made in United States
Troutdale, OR
12/03/2024

25793508R00062